This is Lockdown

M J Mallon

Cover and Photography by M J Mallon

Published in Kindle July 2020 to include my Lockdown diaries

Copyright ©2020 Author Name: M J Mallon

All rights reserved Kyrosmagica Publishing

Paperback ISBN:978-1-9998224-5-3

DEDICATION

To the blogging and writing community, you have kept me busy during this unprecedented time. To my family and friends who keep me sane. To my writing muse: you are my heart, my soul, my me.

.

ACKNOWLEDGEMENTS

I have enjoyed compiling this COVID19 short stories, flash fiction and poetry collection. It has kept me busy and focused, taking my mind off the sadness, and anxiety of this time. I appreciate the writing and blogging community and I'm honoured to be a part of it.

Thank you to all those who have contributed to the Isolation for Writers series. To my blogging and author friends who help me with beta reading, blog tours and the like. Thank you also to all those who read and review my books. I appreciate you all so much.

The writers, bloggers and creatives who contributed their thoughts, poems and flash fiction to this anthology set during the first lockdown in the UK are:
Richard Dee, Catherine Fearns, Lynn Fraser, Jackie Carreira, Willow Willers, Sharon Marchisello, Fi Phillips, Jeannie Wycherley, Chantelle Atkins, Tracie Barton-Barrett, Peter Taylor-Gooby, Ritu Bhathal, Alice May, Miriam Owen, Drew Neary and Ceri Williams,Katherine Mezzacappa, (author name: Katie Hutton,) Sally Cronin, Debby Gies (author name: D G Kaye), Adele Marie Park, Frank Prem, Marian Wood, Samantha Murdoch, Anne Goodwin, Beaton Mabaso, Sherri Matthews, and Jane Horwood and Melissa Santiago-Val–Community Masks 4 NHS/Sew Positive.

To all those who have reviewed and/or promoted me during Lockdown—in particular I'd like to mention: Sally Cronin, Miriam Hurdle, John C Cudney, Adele Marie Park, Camilla Downs, Darlene Foster, Priscilla Bettis, D G Kaye writer (Debby Gies,) and Samantha Murdoch. For two special humans for inspiring me to write poetry and flash fiction: Colleen Chesebro and Charli Mills @ Carrot Ranch Literary Community.

PREFACE

As a nation we were glad to leave 2019 behind. It hadn't been the best year with climate change issues: Australian Wildfires, Brexit uncertainty, and massive flooding in the UK being just some of the reported troubles, along with the Hong Kong riots.

But little did we know what terror 2020 had in store for us. This will be the year that future generations will study in history books, both in the UK and overseas.

From the start I had an uneasy feeling about corona virus. Initially, I suppressed the qualms I felt. But the signs were there for all to see, the protective gear worn by medical staff went far beyond the normal hospital garb. These high-tech scrubs were the first clue that this was a highly infectious and potentially lethal disease.

People were still dismissing it as a flu, but this didn't sit right with me. Flu has a vaccine, flu is a familiar illness (a lot of the population have suffered with it at one point or another.) It can be a killer too; but corona virus was a killer with so many unknown variables. This disease has no vaccine yet, we don't really know what it can do, and the long-term impact of the virus on the immune system are as yet unknown. Also, we had no clue just how badly the economies of the world would be hit by implementing controls to contain the virus.

In the UK we listened to the shocking accounts circulating from China, Italy, Spain, and many other countries with daily totals of the number of people infected, and the shocking death count. The press reported the majority of the deceased were the most vulnerable in our society: the elderly, or people with underlying health conditions.

Although this is still the case there have been cases of young children, the middle-aged and young adults dying.

The sad story of Li Wenliang, the Chinese whistleblower doctor, who warned of the dangers of this disease rocked the world. He contracted the virus while working at Wuhan Central Hospital. Apparently, he had sent out a warning to fellow medics to wear protective clothing on 30th December but police had told him to stop "making false comments." A month later he was diagnosed with corona virus.

And sadly at 02:58 on Feb. 7th, aged just thirty-four, Li Wenliang died leaving behind a pregnant wife who gave birth to his baby son on the 12th of June.

Initially, our Prime Minister seemed somewhat blase—adopting a stiff upper lip herd immunity stance: to infect a proportion of the population so they would be immune to the virus. As the death toll grew this became a dangerous policy to adopt. Our NHS would be overwhelmed. Something had to be done.

The WHO announced corona virus as a pandemic on 11th March 2020.

On 23rd March 2020 UK lockdown was announced by our Prime Minister, Boris Johnson.

The first half of This Is Lockdown includes 'The Isolation' authors, writers and bloggers, who featured on my blog plus several poems, and writings.

My COVID19 diaries are available to read in the longer kindle version of *This Is Lockdown*. They are a personal account of my experience during the corona virus. I count myself lucky. Tragically, there are many families who lost their loved ones in this pandemic, to date mine are all safe and well. Equally, there are people suffering in cramped conditions, living in poverty, struggling with impossible circumstances, wondering how they are going to pay their rent, or feed their children, if they survive.

Please spare a thought for them and for the refugees, and vulnerable women in abusive relationships trapped by this situation.

The second half of the collection features my short stories, flash fiction and poetry written during this time.

It begins with a YA romance short story: The Poet's Club set post virus. Perhaps if it is well received, I may develop this idea into a novella or novel. The other pieces range from purely fictional stories to those that are based on true life incidences and news stories. Sometimes, names and particulars have been changed to preserve anonymity.

Each story is marked with an indicator of genre and there are trigger warnings for any which are sad or distressing, so that readers can make an informed choice should they wish to avoid any which might cause upset.

Having said that, the main goal of this collection is to spread hope, love and truth.

M J Mallon

This Is Lockdown
M J Mallon
© M J Mallon

28th FEBRUARY 2020

I'm sitting in a cafe in Cambridge, England watching the snow fall. A lady crosses the road with a large black umbrella, the white flecks of pure snow fall covering its surface. I am drawn to this image to write a poem.

The world faces so many challenges at the moment: climate crisis, corona virus, economic crises.

Where are we headed?

This is an early piece I wrote on the state of affairs, expressed with a Tanka poem...

White snow falls to black

Umbrellas hiding cold stares

Finding clarity

Sick Quarantine Continues

Media Spreads People's fears

Writers Write-COVID19

Reflections On Quarantine

My submission to <u>Writers Unite Blog</u>.

The theme was: In twenty years, what will you tell your children, grandchildren, or other loved ones about your experience during the COVID-19 pandemic?

Each morning I wake up with a sick feeling in my stomach, that sick feeling is COVID19.

In this scary world we're inhabiting, there are no guarantees what will happen to our family, friends, or to our livelihoods.

The UK Lockdown came too late; the death toll screams in retribution. Under Government Lockdown rules we must remain at home, venturing out for one walk a day, essential food shopping, or medical emergencies.

No cute visitors grace our household apart from a ginger cat. I name him Butternut; he caresses my legs, purring. Cats wander freely, we don't—we are caged animals—we disinfect, wash our hands, and wait.

The coronavirus threatens the weakest—my husband with high blood pressure, my youngest daughter—the asthmatic. Somehow, even when my husband falls ill, he recovers. With no testing, it is uncertain if he's had the virus.

The strain of isolation makes us argue, swear, eat, and drink excessively.

We discuss our hopes and fears, embrace the positive; bake cakes, keep fit, and paint our nails. My poor husband is the lone male, we offer to paint his nails too. He declines! Our youngest daughter Georgina starts a TikTok channel with short, funny clips. I write COVID19 related stories, my usual genre: fantasy seems alien in this strange reality.

Fear becomes too real when my mother waits for forty-five minutes on the 111 number. It is not COVID19. Her face is infected with an insect bite. My ninety-one-year-old father's voice cracks. He calls himself a coward for not accompanying her to hospital. Sad words that I'll never forget.

Mum is safe at home now, away from COVID19.

I pray when this is over, we will laugh about that bloody insect.

In the meantime, we Skype and hope.

A lovely ginger tom cat who came to visit us during lockdown.

Ginger, gorgeous fellow,

rest awhile.

Shade under this my tree

Close your eyes stay still

Keep me company

Who you are I have no clue

A cat perhaps I'd never guess

You have the fur, paws, claws

Long, whiskers too

Don't go, stay with me

The magic in your eyes

Tells me who you are

Who you might become

More than this dream

A whisper in the breeze

Your fur's too light

Fragile, like this life

Please don't fade

Come close to me

You and I. We'll be

Don't leave me

Rest and I will too

Waking you'll be gone,

Faded like the sun.

Forever my kind friend.

I came across this mysterious hidden concrete frog one day whilst walking by the river...We'd walked a bit further than normal, passing a swan with his head buried in the pond life below. He was in Lockdown! We crossed the bridge and then followed a pathway to the left. To the right of us, we saw fields and in the far distance a copse of trees. When we reached the furthest end of the path, we realised we were nearly at our local garden centre. We had no idea we could walk there via this route!

Lockdown reveals all sorts of undiscovered things.

On the way back I looked down to the right of the sluice by the lock at Bait's Bite and saw a tiny concrete frog hidden below the pillars...

A metamorphosis

Is an extremely long word!

Peaceful writer's eyes

Observe a hidden surprise.

A walk, a river, a frog!

And there were a fair few swans! I wrote about two swans my eldest daughter Tasha and I had seen on the river. One was tranquil and the other was angrily hissing at two guys on their barge. The two swans couldn't have been any different!

Here's a short haiku poem about the swans:

Believe this Swan's cute
Elegant fellow's so calm
Near me's no problem

Swan wife's intention
Her whim is to hiss angry
At barge men in boats!

Hoping that this golden dragon might help you escape for a while…
Time for an adventure…

Golden Dragon

Oh,

Mighty Dragon

Your fiery dare,

Gleams in a challenge,

No Childish mask,

Highlights your eyes.

***

Golden elixir promises,

Hang in the air, Lining up,

To slide off the curve of

Your celebrated tongue.

A challenge!

Adventuress, take a ride.

***

Will I or forever still,

Remain in this moment,

Too fearful to slip on

Temptation's back.

To sail the secretive seas.

Fly to dizzying heights

***

Witness the wonder of sunsets,

Smell the sweet aroma of waterfalls,

Discover dry deserts

And tempting temples.

Cavernous canyons,

Concealed caves.

***

Resplendent rainbows,

Rippling rivers, incandescent Islands,

Languid lakes,

Majestic mountains,

Too many splendours

To describe.

***

I step back from

Tempestuous skies.

Foolish, I.

Must I question

What is

When I can do?

***

Trust my,

Ever growing,

Heart's Desire - Dragon,

Please!!! Take me,

With

you!

Life goes on, sunshine, showers and thunderstorms, but such tragedy remains.

The Shadorma Poems

The sun shone

Enticing us all

To play out

With old friends

The rain cried behind the sun

Days after Lockdown

***

Life goes on

Sunshine, and showers

Cloudbursts weep

Death toll peaks

My heart screams behind thunder

I hate you virus.

Keep your heart open. Be kind. Love your neighbour regardless of their colour, or religion. Embrace differences, they make us unique, individual, special and interesting.

This piece of flash fiction is dedicated to the memory of George Floyd and all those who have suffered at the hands of racial injustice, or who have lost their lives to cruel, racial hatred.

Remember, we are all the same.

Jordan vowed to protect his world from deranged, hate-filled people. He vowed to be a braver man, to speak up against injustice, standing unified with his loving wife beside him.

His words: "Racism kills. It divides and discriminates."

Her words: "We are one, we refuse to let the racists win."

After the protest, his wife's creamy fingers cupped his obsidian skin. Her loving eyes filled.

They both wept, remembering George Floyd.

Their thoughts raged no more hatred, ever.

Denounce racism, curtail this relentless boot inflicting suffocating death.

Stop it now, end the pain.

A Different Pathway

A copse

Of trees past fields

I've never seen before

Like tiny balls of knitted wool

Airy

***

Blue Gaps

Vast space beyond

Quiet and still the grass

My mindful feet touching the earth

Six eyes

***

Wander

Ahead, one foot

Treads to infinity

Taking our feet somewhere special

Perhaps?

***

My girls

Daughters with me

Walking in the sunshine

As we move in sweet steps forward

In time

***

Waiting

For something new

A sight we haven't seen

As we turn beyond the grasses

New dreams

***

A copse

Vast space beyond

Treads to infinity

As we move in sweet steps forward

New dreams

And because we all need to laugh, now more than ever…. I hope you enjoy this short piece of flash fiction which won me first prize in the Bloggers Bash Blog Post Writing Competition…

The Queen's Dress Down Day

The Queen's forehead creased in worry, she'd had enough, so many engagements, accompanied by endless rounds of champagne, canapes and caviar.

She turned to her trusted adviser, 'Dear fellow,' she enquired, 'Could you help me? I'd like to be a commoner for the day, to ride a double-decker bus full of beer swilling pensioners, purchase a sale bra and cheap stone-washed jeans. Oh, and I'd like to get to the lowly department store via a rusty old bike.'

Her adviser's jaw dropped as if she had asked him whether he picked his very large nose.

He wandered off, or hid, she wasn't sure. She contemplated chopping his head off but decided against it. Instead, she turned to Google to find an answer. A wonderful site proposed A Royal Dress Down Day with a difference plus a Royal surprise.

She squealed with delight. Her corgis hid under the bed in shock. She sighed; even her dogs were turning against her!

She squinted at the small print. The Dress Down Day promised a Fairy Godmother, a basic bra fit, a guarantee of poor service plus a cup of strong builder's tea to wash down her disappointment. She signed a special disclaimer to say she wouldn't complain.

The day loomed, Elizabeth was so excited! But, being a commoner wasn't as great as she thought it would be. The Fairy Godmother turned out to be a little girl in a tutu who kept on whining. Instead of riding on a bike she had to get to the department store via an over populated ocean on a jet ski, and the pair of jeans

16

clung to her body like a clinging wetsuit.

All very inappropriate for a woman of her age. She picked up her diamond tiara. Back to business as usual.

More about the competition entries here:

https://mjmallon.com/2018/05/24/winners-of-the-2018-bloggers-bash-blog-post-competition/

The First Lockdown
Isolation Writers
Poets
And Creatives

Richard Dee

© Richard Dee

Based in the UK

Some thoughts on what I'm beginning to think of as the new normal.

I'm Richard Dee, I write Science Fiction and Steampunk adventures, as well as chronicling the exploits of Andorra Pett, reluctant amateur detective.

At last, I've found that some of the skills I learned are coming in useful.

Isolation itself is not a problem, as an author I tend to live in other worlds anyway.

When I'm writing, the ones in my head are as vivid to me as the one out of the window. There are several I go to on a regular basis, home to amateur detectives, space adventurers and quasi-Victorian society. Not only that, but there is also always the chance that I might find a new one to explore.

It used to be a bit of a nuisance, a bone of contention with other family members. Now I find that it helps.

Not only that, as an ex-mariner, I was always used to isolation, chugging across the Atlantic at eight knots to save fuel on a big ship with a small crew teaches you a few things about yourself.

There are things to worry about, all my daughters work in the NHS, on the front line, one in ITU, with a consultant physician for a husband, one is a midwife dealing with emergency admissions and the other is still training. They, along with everyone else who is putting themselves at risk to keep us fed and provided with light, power, empty bins and food to eat deserve our thanks and respect.

Things like getting food, getting exercise, keeping in touch with family and friends: things we all took for granted just a few weeks ago are now more important.

I watch the T.V. and wonder if we will ever live that kind of life, with all the socialising and outdoor action, again.

I'm glad that I have hobbies, things to do on a rainy day. Reading, cooking and gardening.

I thought that I would have so much more time to do things. But any task expands to fill the time allotted to it, so there is no more time than there was.

 Not that we were always out and about; there were jobs that had been put off because I thought they would take too long. Once I got started, I found that they were quickly done.

Meanwhile, I continue to write and publish. In fact, I've just had my Andorra Pett cosy crime series re-imaged, with all new covers by the tremendously talented Gill Trewick.

I'd love to see you over at my website: richarddeescifi.co.uk.

and my Facebook page:

https://www.facebook.com/RichardDeeAuthor/

and Richard's feature on my blog:
https://mjmallon.com/2020/04/18/isolation-for-writers-creatives-ar

Catherine Fearns

© Catherine Fearns

Based in the UK

Catherine Fearns has published three Amazon best-selling crime thrillers with Crooked Cat Books/Darkstroke, and she also writes as a music journalist.

Catherine Fearns: For many people, coping with isolation has been the hardest challenge of these times. But some of us have had to adapt to the loss of isolation. With four school-age children and a husband who worked long hours and travelled extensively, I was used to spending long days, and long evenings, alone in my own world. And I loved it. Now I have a house full of noisy people, twenty-four hours a day, all needing a lot of attention. Not to mention home-schooling. And it's wonderful too, so much so that I feel guilty about all the terrible things happening in the outside world when we are safe in our family bubble. But finding time to write is a challenge.

Before corona hit, I was finishing the edits on my fourth novel, and at the exciting stage where I had just come up with the concept for my fifth book and ready to get started. Then I was suddenly thrust into this new and very confined world. It's difficult to get into the right headspace for novel-writing when you can only snatch a few minutes to yourself here and there—you really need long stretches alone to think. But even for writers without children, concentrating is a challenge at the moment.

Are you finding it hard to focus on reading a book? To tear yourself away from the news, from social media?

Low-level yet constant anxiety has become a way of life for everyone. When you're living with such uncertainty, worrying about vulnerable family members, friends losing their jobs, wondering when this will be over and what the world will be like afterwards…

I found an experimental strategy to keep myself writing. I decided to start writing my new novel as a serial, and to let readers experience the process in real-time. I post two new chapters every week on my website, bite-size so readers have time to read them, and I have time to write them! Readers can even interact if they wish, by adding comments and suggestions. This concept actually works perfectly for the dystopian theme of the book, and I have been using a variety of media to tell the story, including audio files, images, video and letters.

I do feel a little reckless, posting my unedited work for readers to see, but it has also been liberating and confidence-building. Most importantly, putting that pressure on myself means that I have to get the words down every day. I try and wake up an hour before the kids, and if I still need more time, I suggest that we all have a reading and writing hour after lunch.

I'm aware that none of this makes financial sense. I may be shooting myself in the foot by making a whole book available for free when I could have waited and published traditionally. But I don't think I would have had the discipline or concentration to write during this period otherwise. And I wanted to offer something, however small, to readers who might just need an extra little activity in their day.

Nobody should feel they have to achieve things during this time of corona. It's ok to just be—to stay safe, spend time with family, read and relax. But my personal coping strategy has been to create a little something every day. And I have to admit that one of the things I'm looking forward to most when this is over is to spend a day alone!

© Catherine Fearns 22nd April 2020

Author Website: https://www.catherine-fearns.com/

Twitter: https://twitter.com/metalmamawrites

To see the feature post in its entirety on my blog:
https://mjmallon.com/2020/04/22/isolation-for-writers-guest-post-catherine-fearns-crookedcat-crime-thriller-author-isolation-covid19/

.

Jackie Carreira

Based in the UK

How is award winning author, playwright, world citizen and huge movie fan Jackie Carreira coping with this enforced isolation?

Is she taking a leap of faith?

AN AUTHOR IN ISOLATION — Jackie Carreira

The day the lockdown began in the UK, I posted a comment on Twitter. It said: "I'm a writer. I self-isolate for a living!" In retrospect, that might have been a little trite; even unhelpful to those who are genuinely struggling with isolation, but the statement is true in essence. I'm used to spending days, even weeks sometimes, barely leaving the house. I even enjoy it.

What has changed? The answer is: Everything—but it took me a while to notice. For the first few days, I carried on working on a new novel as well as a couple of precious magazine commissions, but very soon found that I couldn't write anymore. The planned projects, and even some new ideas, were still up there in my head, but I couldn't get them out. It was impossible to focus and I didn't understand why.

My husband is an actor. I'm used to him being at home when he's 'resting' so it hasn't been difficult having him around all the time since the theatres closed. We're an unusual married couple, though. We actually enjoy each other's company for extended periods of time! We have no children so the schools being closed made no difference, and earning an insecure living from the arts, we know how to be frugal and make cutbacks when needed. When most of our income vanished at the end of March, we turned the heating down to 15 degrees, put a big jumper on, and stopped throwing away that last piece of bread in the packet. On the upside, we're saving a fortune in petrol and socialising, and every day I'm grateful that our lives are not tougher.

So, why couldn't I write? I couldn't work out what I was doing with all the extra hours, because I certainly wasn't using them to sleep. I didn't spend them cleaning the house either! However, I was speaking to people online and on the phone more, and that was an unexpected bonus. Friends I hadn't spoken to for years were suddenly back in my life. The excuse of being too busy was gone and it was wonderful to reconnect.

Then a couple of weeks ago, on the first sunny day in ages, I had a breakthrough…

"That's it!" I thought. "We're all connected." Somehow, we all know it but we so rarely get a chance to feel it. In these strange times, with planes grounded and factories closed and the streets eerily quiet, I was able to feel it in a new way. I knew that I had no personal reason to feel as anxious as those who are in far worse situations, and I wasn't being overwhelmed by the extra responsibility that others now had, but we're all connected because we're all part of the human tribe. And, possibly for the first time in history, just about everyone on the planet is going through the same thing at the same time. It's extraordinary. Maybe some of what I was feeling didn't belong to me at all. I was simply picking it up from this human web that we're all sitting on.

Armed with this thought, and being fortunate enough to have a garden, I took a new pad and a fresh cup of coffee and went outside. Perhaps all I had to do was START. After all, that was the only thing I wasn't doing. I'm a huge movie fan and never tire of watching my favourites over and over. I remembered a scene in Indiana Jones and the Last Crusade… if you haven't seen it, there's a spoiler coming up! Near the end of the film, Indiana Jones is faced with a seemingly insurmountable obstacle. He's on one side of a huge chasm, too wide to jump. He must get to the other side to reach the Holy Grail and save his father's life, but it looks impossible. Suddenly, he understands that it's a leap of faith. He has to believe or all is lost. So, he closes his eyes, puts out a foot, and takes a big step onto…a bridge made of the same stone as the chasm! It's totally solid. He leans over and looks from a different angle, realising that the bridge had been there the whole time. He just couldn't see it from where he first stood. (A dramatic analogy, I must admit, but then I do also write plays for a living!)

Back in the garden, I took my own small leap of faith, hoping that something might come out if I just start. I put the pen to the paper and began writing anything that came into my head. It was just rough notes at first, then the notes turned into prose, then a whole chapter…and before I knew it, I was a writer again. It was such a relief. I've since been in contact with other writers to ask how it's been for them. Some had been writing more, most had been writing less, for a few it had been business as usual. Interestingly, I discovered that many of those who had started off writing less after the lockdown had also had some kind of breakthrough around the exact same time that I did. Did I cause it, or did they? It doesn't matter. We truly are all connected. I wasn't alone.

You might be wondering how on earth this helps anyone who's not a writer. Well, writing isn't just my job, it's what I love to do the most. And spending time doing what I love is the best coping mechanism I have. I would recommend it to anybody struggling with this lockdown, not knowing how to lift themselves out of the fog of it all. Switch off the news for a while and pick up something connected to what you love to do: a pen, a baking tray, a trowel, a paintbrush, a book to read to a child, a phone to call your best friend. Whatever it is, just take a leap of faith—find a way to start and then do as much of it as you can, when you can. Inspire yourself and you can inspire another. We truly are all connected. Put a tiny piece of what you love onto that web. It already has enough of everything else.

Stay safe. Stay well.

© Copyright JackieCarreira 24th April 2020

Media Links:

www.jackiecarreira.co.uk

Facebook: @JackieCarreiraWriter

Twitter: @JCarreiraWriter

Instagram: @jackiecarreirawriter

To read the feature post in its entirety on my blog please visit:
https://mjmallon.com/2020/04/24/isolation-for-writers-guest-post-jackie-carreira-writers-authors-isolation-covid19-coping-advice-inspiring/

.

Sharon Marchisello

© Sharon Marchisello

Based in USA

Sharon Marchisello is the author of two mysteries published by Sunbury Press: Going Home (2014) and Secrets of the Galapagos (2019).

Thoughts About Isolation from Sharon Marchisello:

I'm supposed to be on a cruise right now. But instead of lounging on our balcony, scanning the waves for dolphins and watching the sun sink below the horizon as the ship glides across the Atlantic, we're watching the sun set behind the pine trees in our own backyard. First-world suffering, I know. We're healthy and have plenty to eat; we even have enough toilet paper. We live in a community with an extensive network of golf-cart paths, and these remain open so residents have access to fresh air and exercise.

Another positive: we're getting our house painted. We've been trying for several years to accomplish this task, but the contractors are always so busy. No one calls you back. In the past, we've even had painters come over and give us an estimate, schedule a date to get started, and then never show up. But now, they're hungry for work. People are losing their jobs and putting off discretionary expenses—like home projects. Contractors are happy to negotiate with anyone who can still afford their services.

I've been retired since 2015, and like many writers, I'm an introvert, so staying home every day staring at my computer is normal. State-imposed isolation is almost welcome—it's a good excuse to not have to go anywhere. What has changed about my life is my participation in extracurricular writer and volunteer activities, which used to occupy a lot of my time. I'm on the board of directors for the Fayette Humane Society; our meetings now take place on Zoom. We've canceled our public pet adoptions and fundraising events. Neither my book club nor my critique group has met for two months. My husband and I both are Master Gardener volunteers; our projects are all on hold, and our homeowner enrichment classes and team meetings now take place on Zoom. So, I'm saving travel time but I'm not sure I'm getting much more accomplished writing-wise or around the house. And in an online meeting, I don't feel as connected as I do when we meet face to face.

I write a personal finance blog, Countdown to Financial Fitness (https://sharonmarchisello.blogspot.com/) to promote my nonfiction book Live Well, Grow Wealth.

When I started the blog at the end of 2015, I thought I'd publish once a week. That quickly changed to biweekly. Then a little less often than biweekly; soon it was more like monthly. And then it was just whenever I felt I had something to say. Since the pandemic started, I've been posting much more frequently; there's a lot to say now. The economic fallout from this global pandemic might prove worse than the health crisis. Many of the principles I write about in my book—building an emergency fund, allocating investments among different asset types, conserving resources, looking for opportunities whether the market is up or down—are relevant now more than ever.

My publisher released my latest novel, Secrets of the Galapagos, just before the pandemic.

The usual occasions for connecting with new readers–conferences, signings in bookstores, talks in libraries—have all been canceled or postponed. Amazon has designated selling books as nonessential. I haven't even held a launch party yet. Again, a selfish inconvenience. People are dying, families can't pay their bills, and I'm fretting about lost book sales.

My emotions during this surreal period have been mixed. On one hand, I feel a heartwarming sense of solidarity with people all over the world who are experiencing the same fears and isolation, trying to adjust to the ever-changing norms of social distancing and personal protection. On the other hand, I'm frustrated by the constant bickering and politicizing of the crisis, the conflicting messages we get from leadership and the media. We're making this up as we go along, acting on the best information we have at the time. It's easy to be a Monday-morning quarterback, sit home and criticize the authorities for what they should or shouldn't have done, for overreacting or for not acting soon or decisively enough. We could get through this crisis better if everyone would cut each other some slack and come together. One can only hope…

© Sharon Marchisello

BIO:
Sharon Marchisello is the author of two mysteries published by Sunbury Press: Going Home (2014) and Secrets of the Galapagos (2019).

Going Home is a whodunit inspired by her mother's battle with Alzheimer's disease, which prompted her to wonder what it would be like to interview a witness or a suspect who couldn't rely on her memory. Secrets of the Galapagos is a mystery with a touch of romance set on a luxury cruise ship exploring the Galapagos islands. Her other publications include travel articles, corporate training manuals, short stories, book reviews, the blog Countdown to Financial Fitness, and a nonfiction book about personal finance, Live Well, Grow Wealth. She earned a Masters in Professional Writing from the University of Southern California and is an active member of Sisters in Crime. Retired from a 27-year career with Delta Air

Lines, she now lives in Georgia and does volunteer work for the Fayette Humane Society.

© Sharon Marchisell 27th April 2020

Website or blog: https://smarchisello.wordpress.com/

To read the blog post in its entirety with fantastic images of social distancing on a beach with a sea lion, darwin's finch, blue-footed boobies, and marine iguanas who were not social distancing, please follow the link: https://mjmallon.com/2020/04/27/isolation-for-writers-guest-post-sharon-marchisello-coronavirus-covid19-writers-isolation/

.

Lynn Fraser

Based in the UK

Huddled in a circle of light

I'm Lynn, writer, reader, mum, drinker of tea.

In many ways, my life in lockdown is not so different in its physical aspects to normal life. I work at home, health issues mean I don't go out often, and me and mine are not the most sociable types. The main difference is in my head. I am more anxious and introspective.

I feel I've become like the ancients, huddled with my little family around the fire in a small circle of light. Awareness of the beasts, that paw and roar in the surrounding darkness, is causing heightened anxiety. When Himself goes to do the weekly supermarket shop, I fret while he's away as though he's gone off with his spear into the red of tooth and claw wilderness. Life seems fragile. Chaos rules.

The anxiety has affected my concentration. I'm struggling to read, fiction, in particular. I can't seem to relax sufficiently to allow myself to be lost in story.

Instead, I constantly scroll through news and social media for real life stories that, frankly, only heighten my anxiety. My heart races and I wave my flaming stick at the monsters in the dark.

For the first couple of weeks, I was finding it hard to write as well. This has shifted, but the introspection—looking inwards at my fire—has changed what I'm writing.

Firstly, I'm back to random journal writing—random describes the timing and content. I'm taking my pen for a walk and writing, not to record what's in my head, but to find out what's in my head. I'm not writing every day, it's not a scheduled thing, like Morning Pages. I carry around my notebook and pen and write when I feel I need to. My handwriting is appalling, so I'm not expecting future historians to be turning to me for an account of life in a time of corona.

Secondly, I'm finding writing my official work in progress like wading through waist-high treacle. And, worse, it's sucking me down. This week I reached the point where, without Lassie arriving with help in the form of a horseman in possession of a handy rope to pull me out (I'm thinking Paul Newman in 'Butch Cassidy and the Sundance Kid', but I digress - I do that a lot just now), I was pretty sure I was going under. The book I'm supposed to be writing is a sequel to my 'laugh-out-loud' story about school gates politics and a mum who will do anything for her kids. The wit is dark (think Fay Weldon) but the emphasis is on humour - and I seem to have lost my sense of humour. (I blame the nightly press conferences from Number 10 and the newspaper headlines and the people dying and the people stockpiling loo roll in garden sheds and the fact that I haven't had a glass of wine since this whole thing started in case it compromises my immune system and home schooling and Himself's taste in music and having to wash down my shopping with Zoflora—yeah that's still on the shelves because why would you want anti-viral cleaner when you can get antibacterial—but, yes, you've got it, I digress.) I'm struggling to raise a snark, let alone a full on laugh-out-loud. I've lost my comedy mojo.

So, finally (I may digress but I have not totally lost my way), I'm writing something different, differently. I have a story that has been sneaking around the back corridors of my head for a while. It's about a woman who finds herself and home in the place from which she ran away. It's about true self and re-learning to trust and believe; it's introspective. And there are witches. I'm releasing my hold on real, out there life and letting my imagination take control.

Things I miss:

My friends and the accompanying chat, wine/tea (and occasional bad singing)

Tea in a cafe

The sea (trip to the coast in May cancelled)

Having the house to myself

Taking life/flour for granted.

Things I'm grateful for:

My menfolk (and cats) with whom I huddle in the light

The people out there working to keep us safe and take care of us

Social media to keep me connected

My garden and my writing shed

To still be here

The words.

© Lynn Fraser 29th April 2020

If you can still accept distraction, my novel is called 'The Busy Mum's Guide To Getting Away With It', it's digitally published by Orion and you can find it on Amazon: https://amzn.to/2Y4B7ZB

You can find me on Twitter as @LynnAFraser and on Instagram (expect cat pictures) as @lynnfraserwriter.

Do pop over to my blog to enjoy Lynn's blog post:

https://mjmallon.com/2020/04/29/isolation-for-writers-guest-post-lynn-fraser-cov1d19-isolation-writers/

Fiona Phillips

© Fi Phillips

Based in the UK

In her own words Fiona is: "an author, playwright and copywriter living in North Wales, just over the border from Chester."

For years I worked in an office environment until motherhood and my husband's career moves tugged me into self-employment, dumped me onto a new creative path, and turned my dream career into a reality. My debut fantasy novel, Haven Wakes, was published by Burning Chair in 2019 and I'm currently working on the follow-up, as yet untitled novel due to be published in 2020.'

ISOLATION FOR WRITERS—Fiona Phillips

When the announcement was made in the UK that the country would go into lockdown, there was an initial moment of panic—panic buying, panic responses on social media and that feeling of panic in my gut. It was an 'oh my god' moment multiplied to the extreme.

Schools and colleges closed, meaning that my two teens were now at home 24/7. Workplaces made the decision to close or arrange for their employees to work remotely. Non-essential shops shut up, well, shop. The country came to an almost standstill.

We held our breath and kept our eyes on the news.

But here's the weird thing. In a lot of ways, life didn't actually change for me. I work from home as an author and copywriter. My husband, although employed, works from our home too. Our teens are of an age where they can look after themselves for the most part. The dog still needs walking, which is doable as long as we don't go near anyone during that walk. Life in lockdown isn't far from the way it was before.

Want to know what has changed for me as a writer? My energy, motivation and inspiration levels are at an all-time low. I know this is down to the COVID 19 crisis—the anxiety, the loss, the frustration—but those three intrinsically-linked factors have always kept me going as a writer and now, when I need them the most, they're reluctant to play ball.

So what do I do to cope?

I keep to a routine

If you're anything like me, life in isolation leads to the days all running into one. Having a routine Monday to Friday gives me a shape to the week.

Mornings are for writing. My teens are in bed. My husband is at his desk upstairs. I take advantage of the peace and quiet and ignore the news and social media for a few hours.

Lunchtime is for catching up with the family, ensuring I eat something reasonably wholesome, and probably putting a wash on the line.

Afternoons are for emails, admin, social media and housework.

The evenings are the time to just be.

I don't beat myself up

We are living in a time of extreme pressure:

* the pressure to play by the lockdown rules

* the pressure to not waste the extra time some of us have been given

* the pressure to home school

* the pressure to work from home

* the pressure of knowing we may come into contact with someone who is infected

* the pressure of worrying about our loved ones

The last thing any of us should be doing is putting extra pressure on ourselves.

So, one night I don't cook an evening meal and my teenagers get themselves a pizza pocket from the freezer instead. That's not going to really harm them.

If I only manage to write 500 words of my work in progress, there's always tomorrow.

If I have a sleepless night, I can get up a little later or have an afternoon nap.

I'm taking life at the moment with a huge dollop of perspective.

I take plenty of breaks

If you're anything like me, inspiration often strikes when you're carrying out the most mundane of tasks, maybe washing up, getting a cup of tea, or taking the dog for a walk.

I'm giving my brain as many chances as possible to bring me fresh inspiration by making sure I take lots of short breaks.

When I walk the dog, I enjoy the peace of a stroll through the trees near my home. I listen to the birds (because with less traffic on the roads I can actually hear the birds now), I enjoy the breeze on my face, and I take my time to watch the skies, whatever the weather.

I throw out a challenge at the beginning of my break—how will my characters get themselves into that much trouble, and more importantly, how will they get themselves out of it?—and wait for the answer to come back to me. It hasn't failed me so far.

© Fiona Phillips 1st May 2020

Website: http://fiphillipswriter.com/
Twitter: https://twitter.com/fiswritinghaven

To read Fiona's blog post in its entirety:

https://mjmallon.com/2020/05/01/isolation-for-writers-guest-post-fiona-phillips-coronavirus-covid19-isolation-writers/

Jeannie Wycherley

© Jeannie Wycherley

Based in the UK

Jeannie Wycherley is "a genre-hopping introvert and word witch living somewhere between the forest and the sea in East Devon, UK. She is the author of Crone (2017), Beyond the Veil (2018), the Spellbound Hound books (2020), and the Amazon bestselling Wonky Inn series. She draws literary inspiration from the landscape... and cake."

I was travelling in Sri Lanka when I first heard the word 'coronavirus'. That probably makes it sound like I'm some sort of global jetsetter, and to be honest, I wish I was. But in truth, my husband and I run a small seaside gift shop in a small town in the south west of England and this was our first holiday in five years. We both have to supplement our income from the shop in other ways. He does so from exam marking (we're both ex-lecturers) and I do so from my writing.

I don't think I was concerned at first. I wasn't paying much attention to the news in any case. But then we stayed in a gorgeous hotel near Dambulla over Chinese New Year and it seemed really odd to see all the Chinese tourists wearing face masks. Fast forward two weeks and I flew home with a scratchy throat. Just 48 hours later I had a respiratory illness that knocked me for six.

By then coronavirus was becoming more newsworthy. I still don't know what I had, but I knew enough about the virus that I self-isolated, 'just in case', for nearly three weeks. Unable to shake it off, I chose not to visit my parents at all, until suddenly, people over seventy were being asked to self-isolate and I'd lost my chance.

We kept our shop open through the first two weeks of March but increasingly became aware we were fighting a losing battle. Nobody wanted to shop, the streets were deserted, and we felt increasingly uneasy—wary of people 'touching' things or coming too close. On the 18th March we closed our doors. The government announced the lockdown the next day.

I had a really bad few days from the 19th March. Extreme anxiety, feeling weepy, experiencing nightmares, struggling to breathe at times. I tried to write—in fact I needed to write because I had a pre-order set up on my next Wonky Inn book—but I struggled to focus for longer than a few minutes. With the shop closed, I suddenly had the equivalent to three extra days to write in and be more productive. Instead of that, I found myself constantly checking social media and the news websites, driving myself crazy.

What made it worse, for me, was fear for my elderly parents. My Mum, 74, has been brilliant and remained indoors, crafting and doing puzzles, but my Dad, 75, is a different story. An ex Royal Marine, and prison education manager, he's been around the block and he gets restless. He has lots of interests though, and one of those is writing although he's never been published.

It came about that I had picked up a pre-made book cover, a fun science fiction. I spotted it in a sale; it made me chuckle and I parted with some cash. I don't write sci-fi. I don't even read a lot of modern sci-fi although I've read lots of 'classics' in the genre. But I absolutely love sci-fi movies so I'm aware of the tropes. My Dad loves all sci-fi. He grew up with it. When I was a kid and we went on holiday, he would invariably be reading sci-fi books on the beach.

I write horror and paranormal cozies. It occurred to me that a cozy sci-fi would be a lot of fun and there would be some crossover with my fans and I might pick up some new ones. The thing was, I was still struggling to focus enough to finish Wonky Inn Book 9: A Gaggle of Ghastly Grandmamas as well as editing an epic Victorian gothic ghost story, The Municipality of Lost Souls, so where did I think I was going to get time to write anything else?

At that stage I asked my Dad if he fancied collaborating and I sent him the cover. He loved it and bounced back with an idea. I suggested he create a plot and he came up with just over half (he admits he's useless at endings). Now, I cannot 'pants' to save my life, so I took his plot and painstakingly broke it down into scenes, fleshed it out and finished it off. Between us we tweaked it and divvied out who was writing what and off we went.

Or rather off he went! Like a rocket. This is a man who struggled to write 300 words per day. Now I can't stop him. I juggle my editing of Lost Souls and Wonky 9, with writing my scenes and editing what he's written so that I can oversee a consistent voice throughout the story. It's hard to keep up with him! The side effect is that I've had to focus because I'm doing so much. It will pay off in the long run.

And do you know? We're producing a great little sci-fi story set on Dartmoor here in Devon, with a nod to H G Wells and those wonderful old 1950s serials like Quatermass and the Pit, but with a little humour and some quirky characters. We use Google Docs so that we can both see what the other is doing, and we catch up every few days so I can check that's he's happy and iron out any plot holes that have come up. It's a fun project that we will both be proud of. When we're both happy with it, I'll send it to my editor. At some stage later this year, I am confident we can launch our collaboration and be justifiably proud of it.

If nothing else, this pandemic will have allowed us to work together in a way we might never have considered doing before. I'll always be grateful for that, and for my parents remaining indoors and staying safe.

© Jeannie Wycherley

Bio

Jeannie Wycherley is a genre-hopping introvert and word witch living somewhere between the forest and the sea in East Devon, UK. She is the author of Crone (2017), Beyond the Veil (2018), the Spellbound Hound books (2020), and the Amazon bestselling Wonky Inn series. She draws literary inspiration from the landscape … and cake.

Well, that was a fascinating post from Jeannie. I love how she is collaborating with her dad. There are positives that we can take out of this awful experience and it gives me great joy to share them.

Coping with anxiety and stress.

Hopes for the future during these strange times.

© Jeannie Wycherley 3rd May 2020

To read the post on my blog about Jeannie:
https://mjmallon.com/2020/05/03/isolation-for-writers-guest-author-jeannie-wycherley-guest-author-isolation-collaboration-thoughts-family-cov19/

Link to her amazon page:http://author.to/jeanniewycherley

Website: http://jeanniewycherley.co.uk

.

Chantelle Atkins

Based in the UK

What's Changed For Me?
Nothing and Everything

The outbreak of Covid19 and the lockdown that followed has had a huge impact on us all, but as a writer, I feel in a unique position to observe, absorb and reflect on the changes for me personally and on the society around me.

What's changed for me? Nothing and everything and believe me, that's as confusing as it sounds. The confusion and anxiety tend to hit me hard in the evening, when my parenting duties are over, and I sit down to write. I'm not ashamed to admit I am often now writing through fits of tears. It's just such a strange, sad, scary, hopeful and heroic time. You can't help but be affected by it.

On the surface, lots has changed for me. I have four children aged between 5 and 17 and they were previously all in full-time education. I run a writing-based business called Chasing Driftwood Writing Group and my time is normally spent running after school writing clubs, writing clubs for home educated children and writing clubs for adults. 2020 started off so well for me, with the addition of three new clubs. I really felt like my little business was growing and succeeding.

When the schools closed, so did the libraries, community halls and museums and just like that, I had no work and no income. Luckily for me, my husband had just had a pay rise that almost covered this loss, so we didn't panic. He works for Iceland and although I worry every day about the risk he is taking being there, I am also extremely grateful that we still have an income and access to food.

I'm now home-schooling my five-year-old son, which isn't too much of a challenge as I used to be a childminder and I work with children at my clubs. In fact, I've been really enjoying it. My older children see to themselves and they've been brilliant at playing with their little brother when they take breaks between lessons. We are also lucky to live in a semi-rural location with a huge garden, ducks and chickens and other animals, plus a vegetable plot to keep us all busy. We are fortunate, and I do not take that for granted.

I feel the fear, like all of us. My 17-year-old daughter has just got a job with her dad at Iceland, and although I am proud of her I am also terrified for her. I try to avoid the news in the day and my little boy is a wonderful distraction and a shining light for me daily. His adaptability has inspired us all. But it hits me in the evening, and I can't help sit and consider everything that has changed and wonder when normality will return.

The things is, I'm not sure how much of the 'normal' I want to return. I love schooling my little one and although I think school can provide a better and more rounded education than me, I am going to miss him like hell when this is over. I miss my clubs and the children and adults I work with. I keep meaning to set up online content for them or engage with them via Skype or Zoom but I've had to admit at the moment I just don't have the emotional energy for it by the time my day is over. I don't miss the stressful day-to-day running around. I spent most of my earnings on petrol I think as we only have one car, so I was pretty much running everyone everywhere all the time. I don't miss traffic jams and it's so peaceful now where we live. And I don't really miss other people. I'm an introvert who loves to be alone. In fact, I need to be alone to refuel, so lockdown is not a challenge for me the way it is for more sociable people. I'm actually a little bit worried about how I will cope adjusting back to 'normal' again. I also think the world was heading in a worrying direction and I really hope that this 'pause' in proceedings will make us all think about the kind of society we want when it is all over.

As for writing? There is a bit less time as the kids are here in the day, but most of my writing took place in the evenings anyway and now that I don't have clubs to prepare for, I'm able to get plenty done. I am tired though as I spend a lot of time attacking my garden! I'm probably blogging more than usual, as I keep thinking about lockdown related things to talk about. I find this as therapeutic and hopeful as gardening.

So, it's weird. I'm still doing all the things I've always done, all the things I love. I'm with my kids and my animals. I'm writing and reading and listening to music. I'm gardening and growing things and spending as much time outdoors as I can. Normal, everyday stress and strain has been replaced with a darker, spikier edge of fear that only comes out at night. I hate the lockdown and love lockdown. I want normality back and I fear it returning. I'm a very confused writer, but that is probably also normal for me.

Author bio:

Chantelle Atkins was born and raised in Dorset, England and still resides there now with her husband, four children and multiple pets. She is addicted to reading, writing and music and writes for both the young adult and adult genres. Her fiction is described as gritty, edgy and compelling.

Her debut Young Adult novel The Mess Of Me deals with eating disorders, self-harm, fractured families and first love. Her second novel, The Boy With The Thorn In His Side follows the musical journey of a young boy attempting to escape his brutal home life and has now been developed into a 6 book series. She is also the author of This Is Nowhere and award-winning dystopian, The Tree Of Rebels, plus a collection of short stories related to her novels called Bird People and Other Stories.

The award-winning Elliot Pie's Guide To Human Nature was released through Pict Publishing in October 2018. YA novel A Song For Bill Robinson was released in December 2019 and is the first in a trilogy. Chantelle has had multiple articles about writing published by Author's Publish magazine.

© Chantelle Atkins 4th May 2020

Links:
Website/blog : https://chantelleatkins.com/

To read the blog post in its entirety:
https://mjmallon.com/2020/05/04/isolation-for-writers-chantelle-atkins-isolation-writers-covid19-ya-author/

Ritu Bhathal

© Ritu Bhathal

Based in the UK

How is Ritu coping with this enforced isolation?

Here is Ritu's answer:

Everything seems just so surreal

When will this world begin to heal?

Politics covering the truth

Blaming the aged, and the youth

We try to see, they just conceal

I feel like I am going blind Maybe I am losing my mind

My thoughts muddle with one another

Feelings that I try to smother

But it's just life, the daily grind

© Ritu Bhathal 2020

Coronavirus.
COVID-19.
Unprecedented.
Social Distancing.
Quarantine.
Self-Isolation.
Lockdown.

These are all words we have heard countless times in the last few weeks.

What have they done?

Brought a wave of panic into your life?

Or are you someone who has taken to it rather calmly?

Well, for me, it's been a bit like this.

When we first heard about this strange virus, schools were still open, yet I had students going off sick with mysterious illnesses for a week to ten days at a time.

Then the government called for school closures, followed by social distancing, and the UK version of Lockdown.

I say UK version because, though all non-essential businesses have been closed, we are still allowed out to exercise once a day, go shopping for food, and schools still need us teachers, but in a different capacity; as carers for the children of Keyworkers.

Once I got over the initial worry and shock of what was happening, I got excited. This meant more time for me to get creative, when I was home. Book two has been started but had been languishing for a couple of months, as the business of daily life took its toll.

But, just because you have time, doesn't mean you automatically switch to the creator of four thousand words a day—well, that doesn't happen to me, anyway.

My creativity has been hit-and-miss to be honest.

I thought all this time would mean I could write, do some courses I signed up for but never got a chance to access, more promotion, lots of reading…

The reality has been quite different.

To start with, I am in school on a rota system, so I could be in for one or two days, but I don't know more than a week in advance. And there is the joy of having both kids and Hubby Dearest at home as well, so no time was distraction-free time either.

I sit with my laptop open on one of my home days, WIP loaded up, ready to write up a storm. Nothing comes. I open a book to read. But I can't get into it and put it down after a few pages. Then I remember those courses. So, I manage another couple of modules on a creative writing course.
But no words.
After the first ten days, we were in official Easter holiday mode. Technically no different to the last few days, but I felt, mentally, that I was on a break.
I discovered online writing sprints on several Facebook groups that helped, and in a few days, I did double my word count.

The joy to read came back.

But then official term started again.

And I have now got online learning to do for school too, to justify us all being at home, even though we are still planning work for our children to do at home. As well as still needing to go in periodically.

Another killjoy to my writing spree.

I'm trying to be practical still have work, but I need my play too, which involves reading and writing.
So, I have taken time to re-plan and structure my WIP, and while

doing that, I have got my juices flowing, again, I think.

My aim is to do school-based work in the mornings and use after lunch time to look at my creative projects, be it writing, courses or research for the WIP.

The evening is filled with family time, walks, cooking, reading, watching films and TV, and if I feel inspired, a little more writing time.

I'm under no illusions. At one point I thought I would end this period with a mainly finished first draft, but I don't think that will happen.

I've had up days, days where I have felt productive in all areas of my quiet life, then there have been days where I have barely wanted to leave my bed.

Those days are the days that suck my creative well dry. The days I watch the news and the world gives me nothing to be hopeful about. The days I had that call or message to say a loved one was ill, or had passed away (twice, so far.)

Still, I'm just thankful that I am okay, we are all healthy, and that, in itself, is the biggest thing.

I'll keep trying to write, but I won't beat myself up if nothing comes. These are crazy times. Messing with our heads.

If I can't write my own words, I'll read others. I'll teach myself new things to make my words, when they do come, better.

But I won't stop trying to write.

(Oh, and I discovered TikTok! Heaven help us all!)

Author Bio

Ritu Bhathal was born in Birmingham in the mid-1970s to migrant parents, hailing from Kenya but with Indian origin. This colourful background has been a constant source of inspiration to her. From childhood, she always enjoyed reading. This love of books is credited to her mother. The joy of reading spurred her on to become creative in her writing, from fiction to poetry. Winning little writing competitions at school and locally encouraged her to continue writing. As a wife, mother, daughter, sister, and teacher, she has drawn on inspiration from many avenues to create the poems that she writes.

A qualified teacher having studied at Kingston University, she now deals with classes of children as a sideline to her writing!

Ritu also writes a blog, www.butismileanyway.com, a mixture of life and creativity, thoughts and opinions, which was awarded first place in the Best Overall Blog Category at the 2017 Annual Bloggers Bash Awards, and Best Book Blog in 2019. Ritu is happily married and living in Kent, with her Hubby Dearest, and two children, not forgetting the fur baby Sonu Singh.

© Ritu Bhathal 8th May 2020

The link to Ritu's post on my blog:

https://mjmallon.com/2020/05/08/isolation-for-writers-guest-post-ritu-bhathal-author-writer-poet-blogger-covid19-coronavirus-isolation-thoughts-writing-reading/

Tracie Barton-Barrett

© Tracie Barton-Barrett

Based in USA

Tracie Barton-Barrett is the Author of BURIED DEEP IN OUR HEARTS and a counsellor.

As a counselor, Tracie wanted to give back and help others during this time. So, she wrote an article/blog entitled,

"We Are All Grieving," https://weareallgrieving.blogspot.com/

This is her article which I am sharing here:

We're All Grieving–Support During This Uncertain Time

Welcome to 2020. We're living in a time where there is uncertainty (which our brain dislikes), fear, mounting death and illness, lack of supplies, 24/7 social/news, and isolation, all to fight an invisible foe. If you wanted to create a perfect storm, we're living it.

So, yeah, it's OK to grieve.

We're all grieving something now…

…the loss of a job, financial security, loss of a family member due to the virus, loss of freedom to go where you want to go, when you want to go, the loss of being at home without every single family member there, loss of that trip you were going to go on, the inability to visit a loved one in the hospital, the inability to have neighbors, friends or family over, the loss of identity or purpose.

Or, the issues you were dealing with before all of this came crashing down.

The list goes on. Although we're all "in the same boat," there are different areas and points of view from that boat.

This situation easily calls forth the entire spectrum and expression of human emotion.

It's OK if in the middle of the day, or late at night, you suddenly feel heart-broken, overwhelmed, or frustrated, or livid, and just want a hug. As mammals, the sense of touch is extremely important, particularly to babies.

Same holds true for adults.

–Whatever feelings come up, see if you can really unpack them and get the core of them. If you're "angry," try and see if you can get as specific as possible. Does it remind you of any other times in your life you're reliving from your past? This is a perfect time to dig deeper to prevent out of control emotional eating, drinking, drug use, porn, or anything else that is used as self-medication. My concern is the number of divorces, domestic violence incidents, and suicides that could increase.

–If possible, try to limit the amount of social media and news you allow in. The kicker is that we need to be connected and a need to belong, which social media can provide. However, it can easily suck us down rabbit holes. Personally, I continue to walk the line between being informed and getting sucked in. It's a tight-rope walk and sometimes I fall.

Think of social media/news as a very rich, high caloric dessert. A little bit is OK; too much will make you sick.

–Try to create structure in your life. I prefer the word "rhythm" to "routine," but whatever works for you, try to find it. Otherwise, the days will just run into each other. If you have kids, they thrive in it, even if they say they don't. Those boundaries create safety, which is at a premium now.

I've found it helpful to have 3 daily intentions:· Get outside and/or walk. Reach out to someone via email, text, phone call, etc. Work on my next novel, FINDING HER SPIRIT

–If you're a position to do it, I also encourage you to use this time to do things that you normally wouldn't have time for. Perhaps set a bigger intention…"By the end of the week or month, I will…"

But, DO NOT JUDGE YOURSELF if you're not there. Or, you don't get there. Or, you find that you need to distract yourself by binging on that show. Or, it's 5:00pm and you haven't done squat. That's OK.

–Emotional/spiritual health needs to be fostered, too. Meditation, prayer, watching masses or church services online. Reaching out to others, particularly those who are alone, is important. If we don't find the need for connection in healthy ways, we'll find it in unhealthy ways. Channeling your energy into making masks, organizing Zoom gatherings, community virtual food drivers, anything to help others is a way to get out of our heads. Sometimes literally just texting someone and saying you're thinking about them is enough.

–Staying physically healthy is also important. Our bodies are meant to move, and if we're dormant too long, it begins to affect us emotionally. Also, if you can get outside, even better. Nature and her beauty is so healing. Kids especially benefit from it.

–If you can, find some fun.

Whatever that looks like for you. I love to sing, dance, and play piano. I also make sure to try to laugh every day, too. Fortunately, there are so many creative videos and memes out there that help. My two cats and husband are fodder, as well.

–Take this time to learn a new skill, language, or further develop one you already have. Or, clean out that basement or junk drawer that's been calling your name.

Again, be gentle with yourself if the only thing you can do is get up and maybe shower. Maybe not even that.

In the same way with grief and/or trauma, not everyone is at the same place at the same time. The trick is to stagger our moments and meltdowns, so we can be there for each other when we fall. It's happened to me when I had a bad day, people were there for me. Who knows what the next normal will look like? No one really knows. We're all co-creating this as we go along. This experience brings out what it really means to be human, as the stories of kindness, compassion, and altruism are off the charts. My heart grows in leaps and bounds. My deepest thanks to the medical community, retail workers, truckers, any delivery workers for are keeping us afloat during this time.

I picture it as we're all walking along a path. Sometimes one of us stumbles but doesn't fall. There will be times, however, when we really do fall. Then, we will be there to lift each other up.

From six or more feet away, of course

© Tracie Barton-Barrett MS, NCC, LPC 5th July 2020

http://www.TracieBartonBarrett.com

To read Tracie's post on my Blog:
https://mjmallon.com/2020/05/07/isolation-for-writers-guest-post-tracie-barton-barrett-cov1d19-isolation-writers-grieving/

Alice May

© Alice May

Based in the UK

How is Alice May coping with this enforced isolation?

This is her answer:

Opening the Door of 'The House That Sat Down'

Many thanks to Marje for giving me the opportunity to open the door on The House That Sat Down and show what is happening to one author, in a remote cottage in the middle of nowhere, on the Dorset/Hampshire border during coronavirus lockdown.

Our cottage looks as idyllically chocolate-box perfect as it ever did—before it collapsed six years ago and needed rebuilding, that is—but that doesn't mean that life is any easier inside for us than it is for anyone else at this challenging time. (A quick contextual update for those who have not read The House That Sat Down Trilogy, our house fell down out of the blue one day in 2014 and was painfully rebuilt over a traumatic period of time, which involved living in a tent in the garden; my husband, myself and four children. This period in my life led me to write my first award-winning novel.)

On a superficial level, the main change to my daily routine that I thought social lockdown would bring hasn't materialised. I naively expected that 'a bit more time at home' would enable me to finish editing my latest book. The opposite has—in fact—proven to be the case and I am reminded that nothing is ever quite what we might expect.

Like many, I am attempting to nurture my family through their dramatically altered lives; a role which requires huge amounts of diplomacy which has never been one of my strong points. But, from a writing career perspective, I initially found myself paralysed by an overwhelming sense of loss.

My original—pre-Covid19—schedule for April was chock full of exciting entries. There were multiple speaking events, radio interviews, literary festivals, book signings and even a trip to London to pitch my new book to publishers. It took months to set everything up, but only hours to come crashing down. My new, very empty April stretched before me and mental tumbleweed rolled around inside my brain as I found myself struggling to process the change without dissolving into tears.

With the world so very different, it seemed that the previous twelve months spent writing book 5 had been a colossal waste of time. How could that work still be relevant? I found myself unable to write at all and that worried me.

Instead, I started painting—no, not the walls, although they could do with it. I created big bright, colourful pieces of art to cheer myself up. I have always used painting as a way to express my emotions, it was a massively important part of my recovery from post-traumatic-stress after my house fell down. Recent weeks have seen a resurgence in my reliance on throwing paint around to make myself feel better.

My fabulous PR guru @jane_dean_pr suggested that I put a couple of free art tutorials on my YouTube channel (Alice May Artist: https://youtu.be/p6bHYY4xPl0).

If I am completely honest, I think she was trying to get me to stop pestering her with questions about what I ought to do.

Nevertheless, it was a brilliant idea and has led to some exciting developments which proves that you never know when opportunity will come knocking. Uploading that first video was the start of a whole new dimension to my creative career. Three weeks and nearly twenty tutorials later, there has been a surge in the number of subscribers to my channel, countless visits to my website (www.alicemay.weebly.com) and an unanticipated increase in book sales. Plus, I've had some wonderful feedback via email, twitter and Facebook.

I was interviewed for an article in Good Housekeeping Magazine which was very exciting followed by a lovely chat with Louise Hanna on BBC Radio Solent, which in turn has led to me being invited to deliver paid presentations and art demonstrations on-line to social groups gathering on Zoom. Who knew that such a thing was even wanted, let alone possible?
https://www.goodhousekeeping.com/uk/lifestyle/a31989711/art-beginners-guide/

There has even been a suggestion that I might like to start running proper art classes after lockdown is lifted, which is definitely something to think about.

My empty diary is now stuffed full of new activities; none of which I could have predicted before lockdown, but all of which I am thoroughly enjoying. Which only goes to show that you can never predict what is just around the corner.Anything is possible.
Stay safe, stay well and stay positive.

© Alice May 10th May 2020

Alice's feature on my blog:
https://mjmallon.com/2020/05/10/isolation-for-writers-alice-may-guest-post-covid19-isolation-art-tutorials-writing-resilience-inspiring/

Peter Taylor-Gooby

Based in the UK

Coronavirus: Time to Write

But the Ideas Don't Seem to Come

I'm lucky—I live in a small town on the edge of countryside where no-one's told the Spring about Covid-19 and I have a good-sized garden. It must be very difficult and very hard managing in a small flat trying to home-school children and keep up with the home-working…

As an amateur author everything seems to rest on the ideas coming in my head. I spend many hours remodelling and replotting and rewriting, but it always seems to start out with a vision that appears in my head: people there in great clarity. I can't hear what they're saying but I can tell by their body language what their relation is whether it's conflict or love or compassion that's driving them. It's that revelation that forms the starting point and the passion that compels me to write, whatever happens to the words in the slow process of finalising the script is secondary.

Perhaps it's that nothing measures up to the colossal scale of what it going on about us, perhaps it's that there is enough drama in everyday life and on TV and on the media now to quieten whatever produces the visions, perhaps it's just a temporary break, a lockdown of ideas. I try to start out on something, but find it hard to take the words anywhere and look forward to resuming normal life when I hope the writing will come back to me.

On my walks, I spend time thinking what the world will be like after coronavirus and how it will differ from the past. We must rebuild and we must rebuild better. The pandemic has brought us face to face with so much that doesn't quite work in our world and also shown us the neighbourliness and the quiet acts of generosity and of self-sacrifice that all of us value.

One of the objectives of fiction is to help us understand our lives together, through imagination, compassion and empathy, and to visualise how things could be different. My most recent novel "Blood Ties" is set in the under-world of people-trafficking and forced labour. The characters strive to change or ignore or acquiesce in the issues hidden in plain sight all round them.

© Peter Taylor-Gooby © 12th May 2020

Peter's Buying Links:

https://www.waterstones.com/book/blood-ties/peter-taylor-gooby//9781838594169https://www.amazon.co.uk/gp/product/B01IKW9130/

https://www.amazon.co.uk/gp/product/B01MTYXFII

To read the blog post in its entirety including an excerpt of Blood Ties, please visit my blog:

https://mjmallon.com/2020/05/12/isolation-for-writers-guest-post-peter-taylor-gooby-covid19-isolation-empathy-imagination-compassion/

Miriam Owen

© Miriam Owen

Based in the UK

Miriam Owen is a blogger and doctoral researcher in Marketing at Strathclyde University. She is discussing Isolation in the blogging/book community:

Lockdown—Week 4. In the time it took me to open a Word document to write the title of this piece and prepare to begin writing I received a message that a friend had passed away in London. They didn't pass from Covid 19 but cancer. I had interacted with this person online 2 days previously but hadn't seen them face to face for 6 years. Online they were looking good and sounding cheerful. Their passing hit me hard. Probably harder than it may have done normally because I had more time to think about it, read messages about them online and more time to cry. I reflected as death always makes us do. I felt strongly that life cannot be lived online only as we do not understand or portray the whole picture online.

My research also forces me to be reflective. It is indeed a requirement in my area. In wider terms I need to reflect upon how this current situation changes the way that we as readers interact with the book market. As a reader, blogger and an academic I have been reflecting upon the cancellations of hundreds of book events, book festivals and book launches. All these things that bring the reading community together. The specific context of my research is book bloggers and their interactions within the book world. I was due to travel to some of these events to observe, interview, film and study book bloggers. All these activities are now cancelled. I find myself specifically reflecting upon the role of the book blogger in these lockdown days.

Has their role changed? Do online events fulfill the same need in readers (and specifically bloggers) as live events do. Are people reading more book blogs? Does a blog tour take on more importance if there is not an actual physical book launch? I would love to hear what people think about this.

I have been a blogger for nearly 8 years now. Do I feel any different about my blogging activity under lockdown? I don't really, not in a general way. The reviews I have promised to write remain. The desire to blog is still there. What has changed? I have had the time to do a long overdue tidy of my bookcases which has allowed me to ask myself questions as I unearth books I had forgotten about. Why didn't I write about this or why haven't I read that? The quiet space to read and write has changed under lockdown. My two young children are now around me all the time and need to be schooled. I am exhausted from home schooling, watching the news and being needed by my family. Bedtime is now the only time for reading (if I can stay awake) and if I am lucky I can read a few snatched pages upon waking up on weekend mornings. My writing space is now the school table, when it isn't the breakfast, lunch and dinner table or the jigsaw puzzle space. Instead of picking and choosing what to blog about I ask myself what can I do to help in my community? I feel terrible for all the publishers and authors who have worked towards book launches at this time. I feel bad for the writers who have already spent so much time on their own and had meet ups planned as I know the planned social time is important for them. I contact some of them that I know with offers to write about their projects. I offer to organise a blog tour for a festival that I go to every year. I send books and DVDs to friends. I speak to more people in private messages to make sure they are okay. In my case all these things are interwoven with relationships which have been grown online but have been solidified in person at book events, over coffee and in face to face conversations. Everybody's experience of blogging is different but for me I love being part of a community. Going to book events is like a renewal of vows, it enthuses me to go on blogging, reminds me why I do it, makes me feel part of something exciting and significant.

Some festivals are moving to online events. Some under their own branding whilst others are becoming involved in kind of umbrella online events where their event becomes part of something larger and less specific. Some have had offers to slot specific events into festivals which are happening (they hope) later in the year. Some authors have taken to being creative themselves and doing pieces for their own social media. You Tube seems to be useful—book illustrators seem to be flourishing in the online visual culture. Musicians too. The first few weeks I thought this is great, all this will help me through these dark days. I usually cannot get enough of the arts and really craved online events when I could not get to things because of family commitments. Now that we are in week 4 of lockdown I find it all washing over me as I drown in online events that I cannot keep up with. I am craving eye contact, the smell of new books, handshakes, group laughter, group applause, group tears and deep, important discussions where I see and feel people express themselves. I know there are people busting a gut to get things online lest they be forgotten about but to me as an individual it seems not to hit the spot somehow. Perhaps there is too much online in my life now. Work online, school online, shop online, sell online, browse online, communicate online, listen online. It is all too much and for me it does not feel like a satisfying a substitute for the real thing. The travel, the human contact or feeling the buzz that makes events so exciting is part of what inspires me to keep blogging.

I can appreciate that some people will enjoy what is happening. In academic circles I often see academics ask why do we need to go to conferences? All the introverts say we can do this online, save the planet, still get our point across and I am screaming no! I need to see people, feel their energy, enjoy learning about somewhere new, I like my dedicated conference time and space to reflect on what I am hearing. The same goes for my blogging and book time. The reading/writing community is an amazing thing in general, online and offline. In my experience with the crime fiction genre the community is positive, down to earth, well documented, well organised, supportive and adaptable. It is one of the reasons that I undertook this piece of academic research. There is passion, motivation, kindness and knowledge. Festivals are important. We meet, talk, drink, solve the world's problems, learn and relax. I miss them like I miss an old friend because they help me to understand, get a clearer picture of what is going on and solidify something important in life. So far Covid 19 has allowed me a pause. Within that pause sits time to think about so many actions including the action of blogging. Have you been reflecting too?

© Miriam Owen 18th May 2020

Miriam Owen is a blogger and doctoral researcher in Marketing at Strathclyde University.

If you have any opinions about book blogging she would love to hear from you at miriam.owen@strath.ac.uk

Thanks to Marjorie for hosting this piece in her Covid series. Miriam's blogs are: nordicnoirblog.wordpress.com and walkingbassbuzz.wordpress.com

Thank you Miriam for being my guest. I am so sorry to hear the sad news about your friend. Sending my deepest condolences.

I wish that things could be different. I wish that COVID19 had never happened. I miss meeting my writing and blogging friends in person and attending festivals, particularly the Edinburgh International Festival and Book Festival. But I am so glad that I started this feature—it has been rewarding and given me a focus on something other than COVID19.

I am enjoying all of the articles submitted to me and they have all been so different!

It is by no means easy to cope with this time in our lives. We must try to be patient, whilst we keep on reading, writing and sharing our love of the written word.

Thank you so much for sharing your thoughts.

More about Miriam's blog here:
https://mjmallon.com/2020/05/18/isolation-for-writers-guest-post-miriam-owen-cov1d19-isolation-bloggers-books-blogging/

Ceri and Drew

© Ceri Williams & Drew Neary

Based in the UK

How are Ceri and Drew coping with this enforced isolation?

Hello everyone!

We are Ceri Williams and Drew Neary and we co-write supernatural thrillers. Our first book "The Clockmaker" is a novel set just after WW2. There is a third member of our team—our illustrator Priscila Arandez who produces our cover art.

Our second novel "The Perfect Child," will be released some time after
COVID-19 finally releases us from it's grip.

Drew: The biggest difference to my day in lockdown, is that my children are now at home 24/7. As a parent this offers a lot of challenges but also opportunities. Firstly, the children have to be kept safe, schooled and given plenty of exercise time. I found that establishing a routine really helped—so we do our schooling, then it's exercise time—usually a walk in the sunshine to somewhere green and leafy. After that we have free time where the children usually play and I get some writing done. Then it's evening mealtime and we sit down and watch a DVD, play a board game etc.

I always carry a pen and note pad or my Dictaphone with me during the day. So when moments of inspiration strike, I can record them for later use and they are not lost nor fade from memory. So far, even though my writing time has drastically reduced, it's been quite an enjoyable, positive experience.

There are so many hours in the day, so the writing has to be reduced—but it's always there, on a smaller scale bubbling away in the mind, being recorded, kept in pockets for a later day.

As co-writers, the major downside of lock down is no face – to – face meetings. This, I really miss, but we have to be sensible and follow the guidelines, so it just means more chats on the phone and on Facebook.

Ceri:I am less disciplined than Drew and only write when the muse occurs. It is harder now that we are apart as writers, but we send each other pieces of writing and that often kick starts my own writing process. I am solitary by nature and so these weeks of isolation aren't unusual. But lack of choice to go out, see friends and especially loved ones has been very hard for me, as it has for millions globally.

Us: We greatly miss our author visits to shops, libraries and book clubs. Not only is it a chance to promote and sell our book, but we are very sociable people and it's fantastic to meet and engage with fellow readers and book fans.

There is no real way around this current situation as authors promoting their work. Social media of course—Twitter, Face book etc, are all tools to promote, meet new people and talk but for me it's just not quite the same as meeting people in person.

One of the questions we are often asked on our visits or interviews, is how do you co-write? Is it difficult? Is there conflict? Oddly, it is a very smooth process based on respect for each other's ideas and individual styles of writing.

We both write either independently (and prior to this lockdown) together. Then amalgamate, discuss next steps and repeat the process.

Ceri is brutal with the editing which happens primarily when we are both satisfied that the story is all down.

So at the end of the day, lock down has put us all into our little personal bubbles.

The Clockmaker is the first in an upcoming series of gripping supernatural books by Nottingham based Ceri Williams and Drew Neary.

Widowed in World War 2, Annette and her young son face a completely different life as they exchange the devastation of post-blitz London for the slow pace of a small village. The house they have inherited is old, its bones still settling, creaking noises in the dead of night and the murmur of scritch-scritch in the walls. Located outside the village of Lochnagar, it's been empty for many years.

The unfolding of how the Clockmaker made his plans, his meticulous preparations and macabre creations, all builds up to a series of gruesome, horrific murders. These have just one end in view: his release from that which has held him captive for centuries.

"The Clockmaker is a character in the much larger Novel – Optics. When we put some extracts on our website, we received acclaim, and requests to develop the minor characters further. That was when The Clockmaker was born," comment debut authors Ceri and Drew. The authors are currently arranging a series of book launches around the local area and have engaged various local writing groups with their debut.

A chilling supernatural novel with characters you'll come to care for, The Clockmaker will interest anyone who fears the dark—and what might lie in the shadows...

DREW NEARY became interested in history, science fiction/fantasy and conspiracy theories in his teenage years. This prompted him to write short stories over the years. He is also a fan of tabletop gaming.

CERI WILLIAMS has always loved language, and after a 5 year stint in advertising and journalism, now writes supernatural horror and fantasy.

The Clockmaker is their first book and forms part of an upcoming series. PUBLICATION DATE 28th May 2018 ISBN: 9781788034586 Price: £8.99

Thank you so much to Drew and Ceri for being my guests.

Well, I'm intrigued by the sound of The Clockmaker and the apparent effortless of the teamwork involved. Now let me see, I have a thing about clocks.... and I love the supernatural... I do enjoy a novel set in WW2...

© Drew Neary & Ceri Williams 19th of May 2020

To find out more about Drew and Ceri:
https://mjmallon.com/2020/05/19/writers-in-isolation-drew-neary-and-ceri-williams-the-clockmaker-covid19-isolation-writers-supernatural-novel-series/

Katherine Mezzacappa

© Katherine Mezzacappa

Based in Italy

Katherine Mezzacappa is an Irish writer of mainly historical fiction now living in Italy. She also writes as Katie Hutton and as Kate Zarrelli.

At time of writing, lockdown here in Italy is easing, but I am still wary of emerging into the sunlight. To begin with, it wasn't isolation per se that was difficult to cope with from a creative point of view, but the fear of all the unknowns around the pandemic—I've got a little better at living with them. I had the advantage of having worked from home for years so I was used to not having the routines of a commute and a shared office. However, my job is paused at the moment until later in the year, which meant I had to think about how best to use that time. Time is what writers often complain they don't have enough of, but when you're suddenly faced with lots of it, the prospect is daunting, and you feel guilty if you don't take advantage. I know from my writing network that I'm far from alone in feeling that.

I had final edits to do on two books, The Gypsy Bride (Katie Hutton) and The Casanova Papers(Kate Zarrelli) so having the space for them was a boon, though revisiting a book set in Venice when I could see that city on webcams, silent and shuttered, was also heart-breaking. Writing did pick up though, as well as other 'writery' activities. I've co-presented at a virtual litfest with an old friend from MA days, though we're thousands of miles apart.

I am now an assessor for a writing consultancy and a proofreader for a new Italian publisher. Writing predominantly historical fiction is an advantage in lockdown, as the writer must perforce go in her head into a vanished world, and the less interference from the modern one there is, the better (provided that for research purposes, Google works, and ABEbooks still deliver!). Frustration as a writer lies in not being able to do field visits for future projects—a first world problem, and those places will be waiting for me afterwards. The virtual company of other writers has become more important than ever before. There have been some stellar online opportunities, like the Society of Authors workshops, and the Arvon at Home readings. I hope these persist alongside conventional offerings once the pandemic has passed, as they represent real accessibility and democratisation of the business of writing.

Katherine's début historical novel as Katie Hutton, The Gypsy Bride, was published June 2020 by Zaffre Books.

A sequel, The Gypsy's Daughter, is in preparation for June 2021. As Kate Zarrelli, writing for eXtasy Books, she is the author of Tuscan Enchantment (2019) and The Casanova Papers (June 2020). Her short fiction (as Katherine Mezzacappa) has appeared in Ireland's Own, Erotic Review Magazine, The Copperfield Review, Turnpike, Asymmetry and in anthologies with the Bedford International Writing Competition, Henshaw Press and Severance Publications. She's a member of the Irish Writers Centre, the Irish Writers Union, the Society of Authors, the Historical Novel Society, the Historical Writers' Association and the Romantic Novelists Association. She was awarded a Cill Rialaig residency by the Irish Writers Centre in 2019 for the writing of a Renaissance novel, Giulia of the Albizzi.

Katherine regularly reviews for the Historical Novel Society.

She holds a Masters in Creative Writing from Canterbury Christ Church University in addition to an MLitt in Eng Lit from Durham and a first degree in History of Art from UEA.

You are never alone with a book; that's as true now as it was when I was a lonely teenager. Historical fiction allows us to escape into a different world, and without being preachy about it, can help us realise that we've been through terrible times before without the advances in healthcare and communication that aid us now. I do not believe that writers of historical fiction should offer nostalgia to their readers—more perhaps a realisation that human beings are often more resilient than they realise.

© Katherine Mezzacappa 22nd of May 2020

Katherine's links:
https://www.facebook.com/katherinemezzacappafiction/
https://www.facebook.com/katezarrellibooks/

To read Katherine's blog post visit:
https://mjmallon.com/2020/05/22/writers-in-isolation-katherineme
zzacappa-isolation-writers-authorshistorical-fiction/

Willow Willers

© Willow Willers

Based in the UK

I featured blogger and poet Willow Willers with a coronavirus poem and a James Blunt song.

How is Willow coping with this enforced isolation?

Here is Willow's answer:

I really don't know if writers, creatives, artists and bookish souls cope any better or worse than the rest of the population. In fact, I don't think I am coping all that well. I seem to be busier now than ever I was before Covid19 reared its ugly head. I really find it hard to find time—to sit down and work on my blog—and the family even though they are not living at home, they take up most of my time. If it has taught me anything, it has taught me that my blogging time must be managed, as it helps me, so it must have its place.

Marje: Indeed it should Willow. I am so glad that blogging has helped you and continues to help you cope with your current situation. It's tough and I know you have had your share of problems. The poem which I'd like to feature today originally appeared on your blog in February and it is eerily true to life at the moment.

Willow: "I had no idea then how close to the truth it was, though I do hope the outcome is better than the one I predicted."

The Plague

The planet was struggling it's true

From space it was no longer blue

It was suffering from millennia of wars and abuse

People pleaded for change, no use.

Most people tried to help Earth

They knew the planets worth.

Then came the plague

No respecter of king or knave

It cut through the ranks and top brass

No preference for age or class

It sent weak, old or young to the grave.

It emptied the streets and Malls,

Pubs, clubs and church halls.

It stopped the planes and the trains

The fat cats lost their profits and gains.

Huge nations brought to their knees

As scientists search for the keys

To the elusive cure to rid all of the bain.

Just when it could not get worse

Hate joined fear with a curse.

The people turn on each other

Neighbour, husband, wife, sister, brother.

Empty shops, no fuel they could not stand

Then all civilian movement was banned

The crops and animals died on the land.

Drones flew over head, all was scanned.

Mother Nature watched with a tear

Chaos in weeks, rebellion, extinction within a year.

© Willow Willers 2020

Bio—Willow Willers

I am the mum of three boys all now grown and flown to live their own lives. Luckily they do keep in touch and visit often. I now have two beautiful grandsons.

When I started this blog I had not long come home from hospital after an accident in which I broke my back, for the second time. I was in hospital for a month and had three operations.

It has taken me a long time to recover, I am still recovering but every day my body is getting stronger. It has taken a huge toll on me mentally I had to retire early on health grounds, I had to come to terms with finding out people I thought were friends were not. I had to make a new life for myself. Things I could do easily have become difficult.

Writing poetry and prose has helped me a great deal. I have made so many wonderful friends through blogging I think it has definitely saved my life.

Willows Blog: https://willowdot21.wordpress.com/2020/04/20/

Marje: You have been through so much Willow. Bless you. You're such a resilient, and amazing person.

To read the blog post in its entirety:
https://mjmallon.com/2020/04/26/isolation-for-writers-guest-post-willow-willers-cov1d19-isolation-writers-poetry/

Sally Cronin

Based in the UK

© Sally Cronin

Sally Cronin Thoughts and A Poem: Silver Lining

Firstly, I really want to pay tribute to the health care workers in hospitals, care homes and those who have continued to visit individuals in the community. We tend to forget when we look at their uniforms that they are also grandparents, mums and dads, sisters, brothers and grandchildren, who have the same concerns we all do about what is going on in the home, not just in their place of work.

Also those working on the front-line in supermarkets and pharmacies that have turned up each day, cheerfully, to make sure we have food on the table and medication delivered.

Parents too have been challenged by assuming the roles of teachers as well as playmates for their children in the last three months, and judging by the photographs and captions on social media, with mixed results. Humour thankfully has been sustained over the last 12 weeks, but I do know that many have struggled with the enforced isolation.

What I would like to focus on in this post, is how three groups of our society are going to cope with the next phase of re-entering the outside world.

I notice that there are already articles on how to minimise the impact on our pets, who have enjoyed having their families at home with them all day, and that includes leaving them for small amounts of time to get them used to be alone again. Humans also need help adjusting to the new world we will find when we reconnect with society.

This includes those who have been classified as vulnerable, primary school children and those who have had their treatments for life threatening diseases put on hold for over three months.

Those classified as vulnerable
I am officially in the at risk group because of my age rather than underlying health issues, but I must say that having shopped in the designated times, I probably will continue to do so as long as they continue... There do not seem to be many early risers at the moment with schools still shut, so I tend to shop in isolated splendour, rolling up and through the checkout without any delay. I do wear a mask and latex gloves and use hand sanitiser as well. Once home I get in the shower and wash my hair and glasses at the same time... shoes stay outside for the day upside down in sunshine or get wiped over with Dettol. I do think it will be a while before I discard these precautions, however safe they announce it might be.

However, one of the issues identified, is covid-19 phobia amongst many elderly people who have become used to having their groceries delivered, and total absence of outside physical contact with family and friends. We have been informed regularly, that with the lifting of restrictions there could be a second wave of the virus, and that it is highly likely that there will be another lockdown when the winter flu season starts later in the year. It does not exactly inspire confidence when it comes to leaving the house and mixing with strangers again as we used to.

This is reinforced with the continued advice for those over 70 or with a long-term underlying conditions, to remain indoors with medication and food deliveries where possible, indoor exercise or in the garden and minimise time spent outside the home and contact with others.

Services such as day care centres which provide such an important physical interaction with others, and also an opportunity to leave the house, have been shut during the lock down. Unfortunately these will remain closed until social distancing protocols have been put in place. But, many elderly will still be too afraid to take advantage of them. Those with families living close by will I am sure, find it much easier to make steps towards the new form of normal. But, for those who are living alone, it will be far more difficult.

Age UK is still doing great work with personal visits to the home, and outreach programme online and by phone, food shopping and other activities. There is a comprehensive website covering Covid-19 and how they can help should you feel that it might be of help for yourself or for a family member.

Here is the link: https://www.ageuk.org.uk/information-advice/

Primary School Children
Teenagers in the main are used to living their lives online, and whilst they will have felt the restrictions on their movement in the last three months, they will have kept up their previous relationships and pastimes such as gaming as normal. But younger children, who don't have access to the Internet in the same way, are at risk of missing out on a crucial time of socialisation with others. When they do return to school or start for the first time in September, there will be physical distancing methods in place that are going to severely restrict how they communicate and play with each other. Sitting alone in a square metre in the playground during breaks and in the dining room is not going to help them integrate into a class community.

Teachers are going to be challenged within all age groups, to not just educate, but be the guardians of personal space. And with teenagers that is going to be tough and almost impossible to enforce outside of the classroom. With the younger children there is likely to be a long-term effect on how they interact with others unless their re-integration is carefully managed.

Those with life-threatening health conditions

The health service is stretched under normal circumstances, but with the lifting of restrictions on elective surgeries and essential treatments for diseases such as cancers, there are going to be even longer delays for patients. It must have been an extremely stressful time for hundreds of thousands of people, and desperate for parents with children who needed urgent treatment.

They are talking about an 18 months waiting list for elective surgeries but hopefully those requiring life-saving treatment will be at the head of the queue. And perhaps all the private health beds that were paid for, but never used, could be taken advantage of now to speed the process up.

An opportunity for us all.

Even though I have worked in the nutritional field for over twenty years, I realised that I needed to take a close look at my own lifestyle and diet and make some changes. I don't need prescribed medication, but it is easy to slip into bad habits, particular in lock down. The key risk factors that have been identified for a poor outcome from catching Covid-19 are related to obesity, including high blood pressure and Type II diabetes. These conditions are all reversible with changes to diet and lifestyle, and whilst it can be challenging, it may lower our risk of becoming infected as we re-join the community.

Double Etheree—Silver Lining

I
believe
there is a
silver lining
to isolation.
A chance to reassess
how we effectively use
one of life's great commodities
so often wasted and lamented
yet measured so accurately each day.
Time can be fleeting or last a lifetime
and it seems there is little to spare.
But during this brief hiatus
I have come to understand
that clocks do not decide
how I use this gift.
In the future
I will live
and love
more.

© Copyright Sally Cronin 2020

Links:

Amazon Author Page US:
https://www.amazon.com/Sally-Cronin/e/B0096REZM2

Goodreads:
https://www.goodreads.com/author/show/7979187.Sally_Cronin

Blog: https://smorgasbordinvitation.wordpress.com/

Brief Bio

I have been a storyteller most of my life (my mother called them fibs!) Poetry, song lyrics and short stories were left behind when work and life intruded, but that all changed in 1996.

My first book Size Matters was a health and weight loss book based on my own experiences of losing 70kilo. I have written another twelve books since then on health and also fiction including three collections of short stories.

My latest collection is Life's Rich Tapestry: Woven in Words… verse, micro fiction and short stories. I am an indie author and proud to be one.

My greatest pleasure comes from those readers who enjoy my take on health, characters and twisted endings... and of course come back for more.

Thank you so much to Sally Cronin for contributing her wonderful Etheree poem and her thoughts to the collection. She is a tireless supporter of the indie author community. A lovely lady, who I have the pleasure of meeting in person.

The link to Sally's poem on my blog:

https://mjmallon.com/2020/06/18/sally-cronin-lockdown-poetry-thoughts-isolation-writers/

Debby Gies

© D G Kaye

Based in Canada

D G Kaye Thoughts And A Poem: Cabin Fever

Marje, thanks for inviting me to share my thoughts on Covid19 and my observances. I've written a Double Etheree to express my thoughts.

***

These are most certainly strange times. Covid19 has put the world on pause. These uncertain times give us opportunity to reflect and step outside the box of life as we knew it, urging us all to take a good long look at our world.

Across the globe there are people hiding safely in their homes, people who worry about losing their homes, and many who protest the lockdown rules by defying them.

Question marks still abound about this mysterious disease as there is still much we've yet to learn about the contagious Coronavirus. Countries are doing their best to keep 'the curve' down from spread and it's up to each one of us to do our parts in both dodging and keeping from spreading it in our tracks. But human nature is always a factor, and there will always be those who oppose the rule of law.

I'm a writer, so I observe life and its contradictions. From my vantage point I've seen a lot of the world expose itself through this unprecedented time, from the good to the bad, from the obedient to the defiant. I've seen images of waters clearing and fish once again swimming in places not seen for decades. I've seen images of nature from afar, otherwise camouflaged by smog. This pause is revealing to us what's wrong down to the core's nub of this world. I'm seeing the greed of man and the kindness of strangers. I'm seeing how seniors in many places are being forgotten with age, but I'm also seeing that the next generation is taking a stand in crime, climate, equality and racism, and convinced it is they who will most likely be the generation to save the world. I'm seeing despair, but I'm seeing the hope. The purge is on and we are observing and living it.

There's always upheaval before building anew—first comes the demolition, and from that will rise new beginnings. We are in the moment of the pre-new beginnings. We have one last big chance to keep the movement going for the change to come. The change for last chance to make the world better in every possible way. This is what I see.

As a writer, the isolation part doesn't affect me because I'm always writing or clicking away on a computer, working best in a solo environment. The only affecting part is going out for groceries and having to wait in a line, 6 feet distanced from the next human, in order to enter, and same procedure to checkout. I abhor grocery shopping in a normal world. Covid19 just exacerbated the issue. I am very much missing human engagement—talking in person, hugging a friend, and seeing a compassionate, genuine smile, not hidden behind a mask.

Cabin Fever

Anxiety exacerbates within.

The pandemic reigns on human life.

We grieve the lost art of living.

While idling in neutral,

We remain suspended,

Awaiting normal,

A new concept.

Lessons taught.

Observe.

Breathe!

Bio:

Debby Gies is a Canadian nonfiction/memoir author who writes under the pen name of D.G. Kaye. She was born, raised, and resides in Toronto, Canada. Kaye writes about her life experiences, matters of the heart and women's issues.

D.G. writes to inspire others. Her writing encompasses stories taken from events she encountered in her own life, and the lessons taken from them. Her sunny outlook on life developed from learning to overcome challenges in her life and finding the upside from those situations. Her refusal to accept the word No or the phrase I can't, keep her on the path to positivity. Kaye loves to look for the humor in whatever life can dish out, and when she isn't writing intimate memoirs, she brings her natural sense of humor into her other works. She writes with a rawness and honesty, leaving readers with something to take from her stories.

Social Links:

www.dgkayewriter.com

www.amazon.com/author/dgkaye7

The link to Debby's post on my blog:

https://mjmallon.com/2020/06/13/isolation-writers-d-g-kaye-covid19-thoughts-isolation-etheree-poem/

Adele Marie Park

© Adele Marie Park

Based in UK (Scotland)

A Poem From Adele Marie Park

World End

Rain falls on parched empty streets

A child's face framed by a window,

No school today no chance of play either,

A fraown creases an unlined brow,

Not understanding, but sensing echoes of adult fear,

Something is very wrong in this adult world,

The grown ups cry and they shout,

She turns away from the grey, wet streets,

And wishes and wishes for the old world again.

Adele Marie Park was born in the north-east of Scotland, and at the age of six months, she moved to live with family on the Orcadian island of Rousay.

Her childhood was surrounded by the tales and legends of old, and these became the themes and beliefs she's carried with her through life as they now emerge and live within the pages of her books.

Adele's first published book is Wisp. A tale of murder, passion and intrigue set in the mythical world of Edra.

She has won awards for her short stories and many have been published in successful anthologies.

Her writing crosses genres between fantasy and horror but is always character driven. Transforming the pictures and characters in her head as if by magic onto the pages of her books. Her belief in magic, faeries and the paranormal has never wavered.

She connects with people through her writing and her wish is for them to live every moment of the story and feel as if they have been on the journey with the characters.

When not writing, she enjoys painting and playing music. Her preferred instrument is the guitar although she has been known to play the tin whistle.

© Adele Marie Park 2020

Adele's blog: https://firefly465.wordpress.com/

The post on my blog:

https://mjmallon.com/2020/06/15/adele-marie-park-pandemic-poetry-covid19-lockdown/

Frank Prem

© Frank Prem

Based in Australia

Frank Prem has been a storytelling poet for forty years.

When not writing or reading his poetry to an audience, he fills his time by working as a psychiatric nurse.

He has been published in magazines, e-zines and anthologies, in Australia and in a number of other countries, and has both performed and recorded his work as 'spoken word'.

Frank has published several collections of free verse poetry—Small Town Kid (2018), Devil In The Wind (2019), and The New Asylum (2019). and A Love Poetry Trilogy (Walk Away Silver Heart; A Kiss for the Worthy; and Rescue and Redemption) in 2020, as well as a two part picture book—A Beechworth Bakery Bears e-Book and A Beechworth Bakery Bears e-Book (too).

He and his wife live in the beautiful township of Beechworth in northeast Victoria (Australia).

unknowing (the city)

.

.

the trees

do not care

beyond yellow

and red

.

the stream

does not worry

it just runs

.

for the rains

have come

and the world

has turned

.

it is autumn again

as it should be

.

the city

close by

has died

just a little

.

there is trouble

now

in finding

a soul

.

for it is people

that it needs

and the people

are all home

.

nothing

on the streets

but their echo

.

and a little

lost litter

that rides

upon the wind

whose song is sung

quite alone

.

but the trees

around the village

don't live

city life

.

they feel

for changes

in the air

.

colour

their leaves

as one season

becomes the next

.

if people stay home

they don't know it

.

if the city

is alone

they don't know

.

Author Links:

Frank Prem Author Page (Newsletter sign up):
https://FrankPrem.com

Amazon: https://www.amazon.com/-/e/B07L61HNZ4

Goodreads:
https://www.goodreads.com/author/show/18679262.Frank_Prem

Get in touch. Frank loves to chat with readers.

Marian Wood

© Marian Wood

Based in the UK

Marian Wood Thoughts And Our Changed World Poetry

I am a happily married, working mum to two children aged seven and nine. I write two blogs featuring my children, poetry and short stories. I'm currently working on my first novel. I have reached about 80,000 words and I'm stuck with the ending. I stopped writing it in October 2019 and now I'm struggling to get back into it. Confidence and COVID 19 are not helping to motivate me.

I've learnt If you are writing a novel, don't stop writing it until it's finished. If you stop and take a break it might take longer. I'd have completed it if I hadn't stopped.

For us, COVID 19 has meant isolation. My husband is being shielded so we are all shielding. It is hard not going anywhere and not seeing friends in person.

In March we were both ill and suspected that we had the virus. However, the swab test showed a negative result. This test may not be accurate, so we don't know if we have had it, but we were ill for weeks.

The environment has loved the relief from the pollution. There are positives to this awful situation. I try not to focus on the state of our economy or the mistakes made. The UK is in a sorry state right now. People are still dying daily, and I fear going to the supermarket. Despite an NHS discount, I prefer to order online where there is no

NHS perk. My Amazon shopping has increased as I'm too scared to go to the shops. Plus, we are shielding.

Tesco are delivering our food, Morrison's my husband's prescriptions. I'm working for the NHS from home. It's nice not to have to rush anywhere but I do miss seeing my patients.

As well as working, I am home schooling. The school sends a weekly timetable with web links and information sheets. I do my best to work through them with the children and tick off what we have done.

I work three days a week but due to home-schooling I am working six days. I am exhausted, I'm enjoying it but I'm tired. This week my nine-year-old and I have been learning about the oceans and explorers. It is an interesting subject. So, COVID 19 has brought great change to our lives. Home school, can't go anywhere and mum no longer gets time alone. It has affected my writing as I'm more stressed and I have less time. I'm struggling to keep up with my blogs.

I'm hoping that the rate of infection keeps coming down. At the moment the figures are still too high in the UK. We are hoping that the children will return to school in September as the government have planned. However, we are not sure if there will be different start and finish times, at the moment we can only guess.

New rules in June in the UK have changed the goalposts for those shielding. As from August 1st it will be paused but there are theories of when it might be un-paused. I'm trying to focus on a day at a time, and hope that the situation continues to improve. This virus has come and messed with all our lives; I'm hoping that it is soon something in the past. Someday I hope for a vaccine. A time that we will no longer worry about it and the world will feel safe again.

Our Changed World Poetry

The world is quiet, a new strange calm,
People staying indoors, scared of coming to harm.
Cars are now just sitting on drives,
As people now lead different lives.

No longer racing for the morning bus,
Now staying at home, with lap top, no fuss.
The children are now home from school,
And mum is trying to set the rules.

Sitting working, but watching the kids,
A parent can be successful at this.
With the help of a maths app and a cool pc,
The children can be kept calm and busy.

It was March that this change came to the UK,
And now it's here, it's not going away.
Never before have people been told to stay at home,
I'm so glad for social media and our telephones.

Our children are growing up right now,
They will forever remember what happened and how.
The Chinese Wet Market in Wuhan,
Was that really where this all began?

The children

The children are now drawing rainbows,
All part of our memories and makes our hearts glow.
All our praises go to our NHS and keyworkers,
They are all working hard in an effort to save us.

So, everyone now please look after your families,
Stay indoors, obey lock down, care for your babies.
Maybe have a picnic in your front room,
Or make the chairs into a rocket and fly to the moon.

Trying to think of ways to pass the day,
Bringing in inventive ways for creativity and play.
Make the most of this time that's been given to us,
It's not going soon, this Corona virus is in no rush.

We are not sure when the lock down will end,
But on one thing you really can depend.
The NHS workers are fighting for you,
There's not enough clapping that we can do.

For they will continue to fight to the finish,
Brave and steadfast, their care won't diminish.
This corona virus has become our life's big feature,
However, we need to see the bigger picture.

Our world around us

Whilst the NHS and Keyworkers are caring for us,
Our planet is loving the difference, loving the less rush.
The effects of planes, ships and of the many cars,
Earth's destruction had gone too far.

Looking up now the sky is deep blue,
It's beautiful, lock down was a good thing to do.
Throughout this disaster we need to see the positive,
Reflect on the good, no longer on the negative.

So, hug your children and play your games,
Home school and work, we will never live this again.
Keep your scrapbooks and write your diaries,
And look after your families, and try not to worry.

© Marian Wood 2020

Links:

www.justmuddlingthroughlife.co.uk

Www.marianwood.com

Www.facebook.com/marianwood76/

Www.twitter.com/MarianEWood

The link to Marian's blog post:

https://justmuddlingthroughlife.co.uk/2020/04/28/our-changed-wo
rld-poetry/

Sherri Matthews

Based in the UK

© Sherri Matthews

Behind The Mask by Sherri Matthews

Covid-19 struck and with it lockdown. I didn't jump into baking bread, online classes and endless quizzes on Zoom. Instead, my brain went into meltdown. Then, Survival Mode.

Stock-piling at the supermarket stripped shelves bare. For the first time in my life—in my generation—I worried about finding basic essentials for my family. Lockdown plunged me into my new role as Hunter/Gatherer. I shifted into action.

My immediate quest turned to hand sanitiser. None. Liquid soap then. None. Right. Bar soap? None. Didn't people wash before coronavirus? Shelf after empty shelf mocked me with their special-offer price tags to non-existent products and a slow-rising panic clenched my chest. A rapid mental inventory of the soap I had at home told me we could manage. I keep a spare. Dishwashing liquid works, my middle son texted. Of course, yes. We have that. Never mind no fresh meat, bread or eggs. At least we could safely wash Covid from our hands.

My sons. My adult children. Three of them. My youngest lives at home with me and my husband. Lockdown separates us from our two older sons who live far away. We cancelled March, hoped for May. Then July. Maybe. More like August. We don't know.

Anxious thoughts lace my outings to The Wasteland. But this isn't an episode of the Walking Dead and there are no zombies here. Reality means I must keep safe. My husband too. He works from home now. I am carer to my youngest who has Asperger's Syndrome. Now, too, for my eighty-something mother who needs shielding. Who will look after them if I succumb?

Food shopping is my mission. An expedition for which I need gear. Survival gear. A mask, primarily. It is black. The material heats my breath and fogs my sunglasses. Wisps of too-overlong lockdown hair itch my eyes. *Don't touch your face!* I mantra as I manoeuvre through the aisles and try to focus on my shopping list, blinking hard to clear the blur and people-dodging when they come too close too many times.

My mask and sunglasses double-up as a dark disguise—they hide the stress and, yes, the anger I know is tight upon my face. It keeps at bay those spewing germs from the woman who sneezes and the man who coughs openly as they walk by. It stops the words I want to say but know I will regret. To them and those who huddle in the aisle chatting, laughing, not a foot apart. I need to get by. Excuse me, please. To them I want to say, don't you know this is a pandemic?

Three months into lockdown, food supplies are plenty. Sanitising hand gel and soap is back!

Families and friends can gather, no more than six. But tell that to the crammed in beach-goers and not a mask in sight in the hottest May on record leaving tons of weight in litter, gridlocked roads and major incidences in their wake. How can we win like this?

An invisible enemy designed to bring us down circulates with relish. Will we humans prevail in our efforts to destroy it? Many will never know normal again. Loss and grief does that. We are forever changed.

My normal means hugging my boys again, my family gathered together on that wonderful day, safe and well. In this I have hope. Always, we must hope. And until that day, it doesn't hurt to wear a black mask.

© Sherri Matthews 2020

Bio:

Sherri is a writer and photographer bringing her memoir, *Stranger In A White Dress, A True Story of Broken Dreams, Being Brave and Beginning Again*, to publication. She is published in a collection of national magazines and anthologies and blogs at *A View From My Summerhouse*. She also contributes as a columnist to Carrot Ranch, an online literary community. In another life, Sherri lived in California for twenty years. Today she lives in England, writing stories from yesterday, making sense of today, bringing hope for tomorrow.

Blog: sherrimatthewsblog.com (A View From My Summerhouse)

Twitter: https://twitter.com/WriterSherri

Samantha Murdoch

© Samantha Murdoch

Based in the UK

Strange Days Indeed!

A Tale from Samantha Murdoch

We are living in strange and difficult times indeed my friends, but there comes a time when we must raise our eyes to the future, and reflect and act on what we have learned…

Although not a native of the East Midlands, I find its quirky humour and the people here have grown on me the longer I've lived here and there's always something… well strange going on.

Take the other day for example—as the youngest, fittest and lowest risk category member of my little family I do the shopping and medication run, and I had just returned from delivering essential items to my mother.

"Hurry up for Christ's sake Samantha, you know I can't go out and I am gasping for a cigarette and the dogs are driving me mad for treats!" namely cigarettes, dog meat and dog treats, leaving them carefully on her doorstep and waving to the dogs who were grinning madly at me through the window while standing on the windowsill wearing Mother's net curtains on their heads like very fetching lace mantillas.

I called goodbye and left—"Get off the bloody windowsill you idiots!"—her words of farewell echoing behind me and went pottering off up the hill to return to my own house, pondering weighty issues like should I feed my sour dough starter again—did I need to plant more beetroot and would my partner possibly let me buy a little

goat…

My reverie was, well, strangely interrupted by a somewhat overweight and half naked gentleman running towards me, his hands cupped carefully around something at his groin level shouting:

"Can you do anything with this please?"

Understandably, I backed away rapidly, fumbling desperately in my handbag for a weapon (I found a biro) and my look of confusion must have registered with the man because he stopped running and said, a little more reasonably:

"No, look!"

He held his hands out to me, and nestled on his palms was a collared dove, one of our prettiest native birds. I approached and looked down. It seemed uninjured, and gazed back trustingly at us.

"What would you like me to do with it?" I enquired politely, hoping I wasn't about to be wrestled indoors and commanded to make pigeon pie…

"My cat had hold of it—she's a bogger [1]* for catching birds and bringing 'em in and I can't leave it in my garden coz she'll only have it again, so I thought you could take it with you," he finished, looking at me hopefully.

"Ah! Oh—no, I have four cats," I told him, and we both nodded in mutual understanding of our furry friends' proclivities.

Suddenly, he brightened as an idea struck.

"That house over there—they've got a big hedge! I can put it in there!"

"That's a good idea," I replied encouragingly.

Together, we sneaked across the road, keeping out of the sight line of the house and I watched as the man pushed the dove into a suitable hole as far up as he could reach in the hedge.

We stood back and looked. The dove settled quite happily into its hiding place and we smiled at each other, the half naked somewhat overweight man and I, united in our common goal to help save a little life.

I haven't seen him since, and I hope the little bird recovered too. But in these strange days sometimes that's all that's needed – a little kindness.

Stay safe and well, friends.

© Samantha Murdoch 2020

* The term bogger is the pronunciation used in Nottingham of bugger!

Bio:

Samantha Murdoch enjoys sharing her thoughts on writing and the power of the written word. She entertains and amuses her blogging community with her thoughts and memories, cats, crystals laughter and the magic of everyday life. A lovely blog with a warm and friendly welcome, and lots of furry friends too!

Links:

https://samanthamurdochblog.wordpress.com/

https://www.instagram.com/crystalcats1485/

Beaton Mabaso

© Beaton Mabaso

Based in Zimbabwe

The Last Normal Day

I remember the last "normal" day before Lockdown begun. I went shopping for last-minute provisions, shops were packed and shelves were rather empty, as those who could afford it bulk bought basics.

Some tried to social distance, others blatantly disregarded it jostling people around in queues.

That was also the first time I saw someone with a face mask in public. I did not have one, neither did most of the people out and about. I felt my heart beat faster and faster like I was on the verge of a panic attack, that the virus was here and I was not doing everything in my power to stay safe.

When I eventually got home I was worried about a headache that would not go away, I had a scratchy throat that made me think I was coming down with a flu or maybe the dreaded virus. I tried calling the toll free emergency numbers for suspected coronavirus cases, but either the numbers did not work or they were perpetually busy.

I tried to monitor my temperature regularly but as I did not have a thermometer; I resorted to just placing the back of a palm on my head, on my neck and throat, trying to feel for a fever. After a couple of days I started feeling like my regular self again and was less anxious about whether or not I might have caught COVID on that last day I went shopping.

As the days of lockdown dragged on, I stopped watching the news as the news bulletins had me convinced the world was ending. I talked to my mum more than I have in a very long time and made a temporary prayer to the technology which made communication possible and easy, video calls, instant messaging and of course the information super highway. I cannot begin to imagine how I would have survived lockdown years back when the internet was something I knew about from TVs and the dial-up modems which made screeching noises as they connected.

I remember the first time I had to go out in public during lockdown; I had finally run out of basics and had to do a shopping run. I bought a disposable medical face mask and set off into the world feeling like an explorer on an adventure. I wasn't used to wearing a mask, and I found it difficult to breathe, almost like I was having a panic attack while I waited for a shop attendant to check my temperature and pour sanitiser into my hands before I could enter the shop. I worried that my temperature would be high, I could feel beads of perspiration pop up on my forehead and was relieved when after what felt like forever I was waved into the shop; a cold globule of hand sanitiser poured into my hand.

For the longest of time we have been 'life on hold' waiting as if a day will come when we wake up to an announcement that Corona Virus is over and life can now resume. It looks like covid-19 will be amongst us for a long time to come and a life of social distancing and all sorts of precautions is the new normal.

There's now mandatory wearing of face masks and if you do not have one in public, you may face imprisonment or a payment of a fine. I have gotten used to wearing face masks and when for a second I forget to wear mine, I feel like I have a panic attack starting…

Welcome to the new normal, I could be smiling right now but you cannot see it behind the mask.

© Beaton Mabaso 2020

Bio:

Beaton is a digital storyteller from Zimbabwe who writes on the beauty and chaos of the place he calls home, celebrating the magic and mystery of his ancestry. When he is not weaving a web of words on BecomingTheMuse.net he is the builder of the African Bloggers Community, growing and shaping the African blogging sphere into one that owns and honours the African Narrative.

Links:

https://becomingthemuse.net/2020/04/09/of-freedoms-symmetry/

https://becomingthemuse.net/2020/06/17/of-musical-chairs-with-african-presidents/

Anne Goodwin

© Anne Goodwin

Based in the UK

This is Lockdown Flash Fiction Pieces

Feeding bodies, feeding minds

Although overqualified for retail, this was her dream job. Five floors of books and hordes of readers, hungry for literary advice. As the virus bloomed, so did sales, until non essentials were forced to close. But she soon found lockdown's silver lining in endless days communing with her own bookshelves.

She read in the bath, on the patio, in the snaking supermarket queue, but covid leached her focus away. Abandoning Moby Dick in her trolley, she approached a security guard. From a distance of two metres, she begged to be allowed inside. Soon her PhD (in creative writing) had charge of a checkout, helping to keep the nation fed.

https://annegoodwin.weebly.com/annecdotal/do-you-read-differentl y-in-anxious-times

Police, fire or ambulance?

What service, please?

We'll need a fire ladder to access the roof and an ambulance in case he's injured … I don't think a crime has been committed but what was he doing up there?

Okay, let's get this straight: there's a man on your roof? You don't think he's a burglar, but he might be incapacitated and need help to get down?

Almost.

Almost?

It's not a man.

Makes no odds whether they identify as male, female or non-binary, if a person's in trouble …

I wouldn't anthropomorphise.

Pardon?

It's a rabbit.

A rabbit. On your roof? How long have you been self-isolating, madam?

https://annegoodwin.weebly.com/1/post/2020/03/silver-linings-9-good-things-about-the-coronavirus-pandemic.html

Human cargo

The body to my right had stopped breathing but the left one still groaned. I tried to comfort him but my words were babble to his ears. Too late, the white man taught me skin speaks stronger than tribe.

When they unshackled us, I expected new neighbours, but they hauled me to my feet, strapped a carcass to my back and whipped me up the ladder to the deck. My head span, the boat swayed, sea spray slashed my wounds. Parched, skeletal, unmuscled, I summoned strength to save myself and toss my brothers to the deep. You might call me complicit, but I swore to haunt each generation until they learnt that black lives matter as much as white.

https://annegoodwin.weebly.com/1/post/2020/06/racism-entitlem ent-and-political-protest-in-the-age-of-covid.html

Divided loyalties

Tradition deemed only white boys touched the tuck-shop cash-box; the maharaja would be proud to see Rishi clutch the key. He dreamt of building gold and silver pyramids, until plague confined juniors to the dorm. As they hadn't lost their appetites for sweetmeats, Rishi would have happily delivered to their beds. But, with fagging outlawed by the virus, they'd no way to earn the coin to pay.

"Handouts?" said Boris. "Rewarding them for playing wag?"

"We've stock to shift," said Rishi. "Consider it a loan."

Boris rubbed his hands. "Which they'll repay with interest?"

"Eventually." Yet Rishi felt conflicted: how could he choose between the brown boys who were dying and the club he yearned to join?

https://annegoodwin.weebly.com/1/post/2020/05/on-rescuing-and -burnout-are-you-trying-to-save-the-world.html

Remember Those Thursdays

When this is over

Will you remember those Thursdays

When you poured from your homes

Paused on your doorsteps

Poised to mark your support

With your hands?

Will you remember how,

In common cause with your neighbours,

Albeit socially distanced

In your separate booths,

You fisted your pens

To place your cross

In the box

For the party that promised

To purge this nation

Of the Hydra-headed pox

Of socialism?

Will you remember

Electing a government

That rejected a pay rise for nurses

Was hostile to migrants

Stockpiled missiles not masks

Concreted over green spaces

Sneered at health and safety legislation

Privatised social care

And, bit by bit, sold off the NHS?

© Anne Goodwin 2020

http://pendemic.ie/remember-those-thursdays-a-poem-by-anne-goo dwin/

Author Bio:

Anne Goodwin's debut novel, *Sugar and Snails* was shortlisted for the 2016 Polari First Book Prize. Her second novel, *Underneath*, was published in 2017. Her short story collection, *Becoming Someone,* on the theme of identity, was published in November 2018. A former clinical psychologist, Anne is also a book blogger with a particular interest in fictional therapists.
Website: annegoodwin.weebly.com

Jane Horwood

& Melissa Santiago-Val

© Jane Horwood & Melisssa Santiago-Val

Based in UK

This Is Lockdown

At the beginning of lockdown Haslingfield-based creative friends Jane Horwood and Melissa Santiago-Val began making community-use face masks from their kitchen tables.

It all began when Jane's husband, Robert, asked her to make him a couple of face masks. After posting them on Facebook along with DIY instructions and a message to say that if people felt it was beyond their capabilities, she would be happy to make a mask for them, she suddenly received a deluge of orders. It took her by surprise, but she had a few friends in the village who sewed so she asked if they would be interested in helping.

One of these friends was Melissa, furloughed from the Stephen Perse Foundation. Jane remembers Melissa being hesitant about how much help she could offer because she was working on a cushion at the time. Two days later Melissa had produced 20 masks but more orders were flooding in.

We decided to call ourselves #CommunityMasks4NHS as we were raising funds for NHS Charities Together and set up a Just Giving page with a target of £500. Within days we had exceeded this target and by the beginning of May we had raised £5,000 with no sign of orders slowing down.

The response from people purchasing the face masks was so positive. They were not only reordering themselves but telling friends and family. The power of social media took over and, as the orders escalated, we needed to (in the words of our Government) ramp up production.

Enter our Sewing Bees. A call out to people in the village and beyond brought in washers, cutters, sewers, and elastic threaders. Fabric arrived through the post from friends who lived further afield or could not contribute physically to the venture.

We really felt that our project hit a chord and it showed what a community pulling together could achieve. It seemed to give focus in this strange and new world of lockdown.

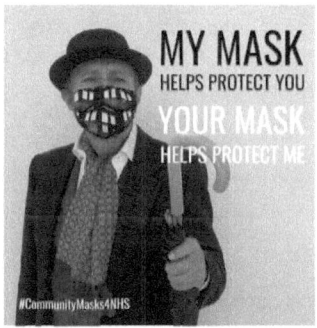

Initially we had been using our own stashes of fabric but this soon began to run out. Friends started dropping bags of cloth on our doorsteps, and the hunt for elastic—which turned out to be a rare commodity indeed—began.

We contacted a couple of local haberdasheries, Backstitch and the Cambridge Fabric Company, who kindly offered us discount on fabric and other supplies. But we were still having to fund the purchase of materials ourselves.

A Crowdfunding page allowed us to raise money specifically for this purpose and we also secured two corporate funders: Johnson Matthey and Metropolitan Thames Valley Housing. A bonus of the corporate sponsorship was that we were able to donate masks to charities and organisations including: Jimmy's, Illuminate, Break, Homestart, Corman's Fields, Cambridge Women's Aid, Royston Community Transport Scheme, and Carers Count.

Other collaborations took place. Dragon's Den entrepreneur company BeeBee Wraps donated some of the vibrant fabrics they use for their eco-friendly reusable food wraps. Fabric designer Deborah at IslandFifty8 provided the unique fabric we used to make face masks for Provenance Restaurant in Whittlesford.

While the first few masks were collected from our doorsteps by locals, we were soon posting out all over the country and overseas including Australia, Spain, Italy, Japan and the US. We've even reached a few celebrities like Craig Revel Horwood (Strictly Come Dancing judge)

and novelist Lucy Hawking.

Our project has managed to generate a fair bit of press coverage over the last few months through Velvet Magazine, Cambridge Independent and an interview on Cambridge 105 Radio.

We even made a documentary with Cambridge-based Dragonlight Films which captures our incredible journey perfectly.

At last count we have made 6,500 masks, used 285 metres of muslin, 4,500 metres of elastic and raised £27,700. By the time this book is published these figures will be out of date.

© Jane Horwood and Melissa Santiago-Val

BIOGRAPHIES:

JANE HORWOOD

Jane is a web designer and has been running her own agency Catfish Web Design for 20 years. In various past lives she has worked in advertising, set up her own fashion label MAMA OCLO in the early 80s (even selling to Harrods), been a painter and decorator, a cook in a bistro, and ran The New End Theatre in London for 5 years. She is the ultimate busy bee. When she moved to Cambridge 15 years ago she set up Cambridge Women, a popular and successful monthly networking event for self employed women. Her hobby is Trash Chic where she sells cushions made from vintage scarves.

MELISSA SANTIAGO-VAL

Melissa has worked in marketing across corporate, charitable and education sectors for over 25 years. In various past lives she has worked at a Marketing B2B agency, as a Speedo swimwear model, marketing a major disability charity, running celebrity events in a school, and producer for a theatre company. She is a fellow busy bee with Jane, learning from the master herself. Her hobbies include meditation, sewing (still learning) and attempting to read the growing pile of books by her bedside.

LINKS:

Our Just Giving page Crowdfunding page:

https://www.justgiving.com/crowdfunding/communitymasks4nhs

Documentary:
https://www.youtube.com/watch?v=rTqjO-kAV0I&feature=emb_logo

Facebook page: https://www.facebook.com/SewPositiveCharity

Part Two

Flash Fiction, and Poetry

©M J Mallon

Poets Club YA romance

I'm Zoe by the way and the guy with the pen and expressive eyebrows is Dan.

Dan and I are in my room sitting on the floor. The bed is off limits as Strictly is lying on it, acting like our doggy chaperone. I'm hoping he falls asleep so Dan and I can make out. Otherwise, he'll probably bark and give us away.

Strictly has just come back from his walk and is snoozing happily. I know what you're thinking, why call a dog Strictly? My mum Stella teaches ballroom dancing, so our poodle is named after the TV show Strictly Come dancing. It's obligatory—dancing, I mean. Everyone in our family dances! Strictly follows mum's routines and joins in. I do too. But ballroom dancing isn't my thing, ballet's more me. I like standing on tiptoes!

Dan doesn't dance, but his eyebrows do, especially when he's pleading. He's pleading now, his arched eyebrows are saying, "Dance for me!"

I stand up, open my bedside drawer to reach in to get my ballet pumps out. They were pink, but now they're all grubby. I'd like a new pair, but mum can't afford it. My hopping about awakens Strictly. Damn. Never mind, Dan and I can make out later! I place my feet in first position. Strictly barks, jumps off the bed and tries to join in, I shoo him away. By now I'm balancing on pointe. Strictly returns to his comfy position on the bed, he sniffs the air with his wet nose as if to say, "If I can't join in I might as well nap." His brown eyes close, sad.

Dan watches me as I dance, his eyes are dancing too.

"Now that your pooch *Stricklin* is sleeping, I want to ask you something," says Dan, blinking as he opens and closes his dancing eyes. I give him a look that says stop calling my dog *Stricklin*, but Dan doesn't acknowledge it. He seems nervous, and scratches his chin.

"Go on," I urge, my voice steps an octave higher as curiosity makes my ballet pumps flatten.

Dan shrugs, thinking better of it. Then, he stands up as if he needs an imaginary soap box to say what he intends.

He hops from foot to foot and then he says, "Let's start a… club."

His eyebrows are arched, one is tiptoeing higher than the other.

"What kind of club?" I ask, pulling a face.

"The impoverished poets society."

I laugh. He sits down, deflated. "Sorry, I didn't mean to laugh but being an *improvised* poet doesn't sound much like fun."

"Not *improvised*, impoverished," he corrects. "No acting needed! Only extremes of poverty and social isolation are allowed."

He lifts his pen and twirls his answer on an invisible pad. "Who needs money, or company when you can write poetry?"

When I don't reply he stands up and delivers a poem.

Let us dine on poetry,

Eat words of love,

And entwine together,

In the divine.

His black eyes lock on mine, and my heart pirouettes. Giddy, I take a deep breath trying to calm my beating heart.

"Come here," he murmurs, his eyes darkening. His hair frames his face in a wild dance. His face is a jungle. I can feel heat rising in my body.

I reply:

Oh this heat,

It sways like waves,

Intoxicating - an ocean,

Kiss me, forever.

He leans towards me, pulls me close. Our faces are centimeters apart. Feeling his proximity hurts me, I can't breathe. I know what's coming, but when his lips touch mine, I forget everything. Everything but the pressure of his lips on mine, the sweetness. The longing. Each kiss is deeper. Different—like a seal. Like I belonged to more than him—to the poetry.

We draw apart, reluctantly. I almost gasp as a memory returns, when kissing wasn't allowed, not in isolation, not when the deadly virus was claiming lives. A horrible memory. One I long to erase. He pushes a stray lock of my mid-length black hair away from my face.

He stares at me. I stare back, wondering what he's going to do, or say next.

"Your hair is cute, Bunches. Too cute. I guess you get teased for wearing it in bunches?"

"If anyone dares to tease me, I punch them before they do it again." I laugh, but deep inside it hurts. I remember what it was like after the death toll fell, after we returned to school. How the caged kids behaved on release.

"Bunches!" he yells, his face creasing around his eyes with the need to tease me.

I whack him, playful. He smiles.

"I believe you!" he grabs me, tickling me. I screech and yell, pushing him back. "*I know you can punch*. I know that about you, you're fierce, Bunches."

"What do you mean?" I reply, pulling away from the need to either whack him, or jump his bones.

"You're different from anyone I've ever known. Purple and orange and black. No one like you. Different and beautiful. But other kids don't like that."

Purple and orange and black. To some girls that might sound like a horrible bruise, or a plague, but to me that sounded beautiful. Those

125

were my colours; the ones I chose to wear, or to carry. Even my rucksack was bright orange.

"Other kids don't get my strangeness. But you do," I reply. "Your weird compliments make me smile."

The air fills with our silence.

I fear it. Like I'd feared death.

And isolation.

I long to tell him he's different and beautiful too, but the words stick like colour on my tongue. So, instead I kiss him, my tongue searching his to tell him what lies hidden in my heart. The kiss lasts so long it's as if it has become the first kiss we've ever had.

As we draw apart, he smiles a cheeky grin. "You've passed the club initiation, you are now Bunches, the poet."

I punch him hard in his taut belly but he doesn't complain, he takes it.

Then his face changes. His forehead creases. "This club has rules. Neither of us do social media. We're not social, we're poets. No insta, *no nothing*."

I can hear the word *nothing* ringing in my ears.

"Great," I reply, meaning it.

"I call you Bunches the poet, but I don't ever do that in public. *That's our secret.* You need to name me too. What do you want to call me?" he asks.

I can't speak. I'm lost for words. I sigh, inadequate.

"It's okay, I get it. That happens. Thoughts and words get muddled and trapped. Once you know you'll tell me."

He hugs me then.

So, it's just me and Dan. A small club for two. Small and familiar. I'm home schooled so likewise it's just me, mum and Strictly. It didn't use to be like that. I used to have a life, friends, a dad. But not anymore. Not since the virus.

Dan's different, he ventures out, goes to work and hangs out at a regular school with other kids but he doesn't mix much.

I look at him searchingly. I can't help but imagine him by his locker, poetic, his eyes dreamily focusing on some faraway idyll, lost in silent words, a contemplation of syllables, metre and rhyme. The kids pause as they walk past him, they point, their fingers laugh.

Every day one kid stops, ready to kick off, they ridicule him.

I don't name these creatures. Naming bullies gives them power. Even repeating what they say seems wrong. It makes me die a little inside.

But…

I imagine one. I don't know his name or anything about him, but I can see him as if his face is right in front of me.

He is tall, wiry, his eyes flash with hate. "What you doing Dan? Forgotten who you are? You're too pretty to be a boy. You've got long curly eyelashes like a girl. Been using mascara? Hair straighteners?" he goads.

Dan's hair is pretty. It is jet black, shiny and straight as black silk. It's long, made that way, as if he was born with his hair reaching downwards. He's beautiful, I say to myself, but this idiot bully can't hear kindness. Bullies only hear cruel words.

Dan's response is slow. Unplanned. He glances at the unnamed kid, who I call No Soul, as if he is a blimp in his day and walks on.

"Hey, I'm talking to you pretty boy!" No Soul says angrily.

"I ain't so pretty," Dan turns, his fists painting No Soul's face with exclamations of anger. Bruises flourish in purple, orange and black.

Each day repeats different bullies and new bruises.

We're a pair, Dan and I, the bullies don't win. They're invisible. They are the No Souls.

But then... it stops. Something happens. Dan doesn't mention the bullies. He doesn't tell me about the fights. And little by little his poems become darker and shorter until they disappear altogether. He refuses to write a word. This disturbs me. I ask him what's going on, but he remains silent. He refuses to tell me.

Our kisses stop, I feel lost and alone. Dark shadows crowd under his eyes. I doubt he's sleeping.

I hate that the No Souls have stolen Dan from me.

I have to make Dan better so I do something which is so unlike me, I reach out beyond my circle of me, Dan, Mum and Strickly. I push back my anxiety. It makes me sick to the stomach but do. I go to see a fortune teller! I'm not sure if I believe it will work, but I try.

The fortune teller doesn't wear bangles, she isn't wearing a headscarf. She looks like my mum's best friend, Alice. Her hair is cut in a tidy bob, her eyebrows are plucked and her dress sense is middle-aged frumpy. I couldn't tell her apart from a crowd of other mums, except for her makeup. Her eyeshadow is like a rainbow. Her lips a painted plum. She pours me a cup of herbal tea and asks me for twenty pounds so she can read my palm. I have it in small change which I raided from a piggy bank hidden under my bed. She frowns a little at the mountain of change but asks me whether I want sugar in my tea.

"No thanks," I reply.

She smiles as if not wanting sugar is a positive. Gathering up the pennies, she doesn't complain, or bother counting it. I like her already. She holds my hand in hers and for a moment I remember how dangerous touching used to be. Even now I feel the fear. I have this desperate urge to pull back and reach for hand gel. She stares at my fingertips but says nothing. For a moment I am convinced she is about to go to sleep. I imagine her yawning. She turns my hand over and studies my palm. Her smooth forehead is gone, now she is a mass of thought lines. But as it smooths, her worry lines disappear leaving me to focus on her eyes which sparkle.

She says, "Thunder is coming. It will bring Dan back to you. If you are both brave enough to sit beneath a certain tree, thunder will bring his stolen words."

"Thunder," I croak. "Why thunder?"

She smiles. "Don't underestimate yourself. Love can make you do anything. Even if the fear of death has grown in your heart. Even if the virus has made your anxiety blossom. The No Souls seek out weakness. You must find the tree of life; it will keep you and Dan safe."

I push back my chair. I stare at her for a moment, studying her face, wondering if she is fake. I decide she is. I leave disgruntled. Wishing that I could have my twenty quid back to buy a pizza carry out. She's already moving the tea things away, making it clear it is time for me to leave...

Nothing happens for days, Dan gets worse. I ask him to come round but he hardly moves from his bed. His mum keeps ringing me, asking me if Dan's alright, as if it's my fault somehow.

Then, I feel this pressure. Tension headaches. Strictly sniffs the air and looks terrified. This makes me decide that perhaps the palm reader was right. I wish I'd asked her more about the tree of life. How could I find it? What does it look like?

The storm is so sudden that I wonder if the fortune teller has arranged it especially for us. Strictly hides under my bed and refuses to come out. I want to join him, but I know I can't. I gulp. Fear trembles through every pore of my body, but I know I must face it. I must do it for Dan.

I pick up my mobile, my hands trembling. "Please Dan, I need you to come round."

"In this storm?" he asks, but it is not a question.

I know his answer will be yes.

It only takes him twenty minutes to arrive; he lives a short bus journey away.

When he arrives he stands in the hallway for a moment saying nothing, inches apart we stare at each other. He reaches forward to touch my arm as if to pull me to him.

"You're a nutter," he murmurs.

"So are you," I reply.

"This is your way to drag me out of my bed," he laughs. "And then back in bed! You, clean sheets plus the added charm of a raging storm."

We hug, saturating ourselves in soggy raindrops. He releases me, and we head up to my bedroom. He tumbles on the bed, his mid-length hair shakes sending raindrops to soak my sheets. Somehow, I don't mind. He motions for me to join him. I jump on his belly making him gasp.

"Hey, cruel girl what you doing!" he says, winded, clutching his stomach.

I pull up his shirt and plant delicate kisses around his belly button. He grabs me closer, trying to unbutton my jeans. They are high waisters. "I love this part of you, your cute love blubber," he plants tiny kisses making my belly button quiver.

I look at my almost flat stomach, "No one's ever called my stomach that before."

We both giggle and kiss. Time has no meaning until reluctantly we break apart.

I look out the window, the lightning is cracking open the sky like a dare.

I say something, words I never thought I would. "Let's go."

"Where?" he asks.

"For a walk in the storm."

He looks at me as if I'm a lunatic. Perhaps I am. But his eyes brighten as if a stray lightning bolt has come to rest in his irises. Shrugging, he grabs his coat. We leave as claps of lightning illuminate the sky.

We walk side by side, silent. I'm searching for something, but I don't know what. Then I spot a tree in the park, unafraid, it is seeking the thunder. I've never seen it before, or perhaps I have never noticed it. The tree is situated next to a park bench. I point at the bench and suggest that we sit down. We sit together but we are not alone. A few passersby rush by, desperate to get home. How strange, during Lockdown everyone was desperate to get out. Our homes became our prisons. And now...

No one would approve of us sitting here, paying no regard to nature. The tree adopts a scowling face. I wonder if it's face is a bad ass omen.

Dan's clothes are as sodden as mine. But we don't mind. My bunches cling to my face. He stares at his feet and presses his rubber soles into the electrocuted puddles.

He stamps down hard splashing in the puddles. I don't tell him to stop. I'm waiting, waiting for him to say something.

"I can't write anymore," he groans. "That's why I've been hiding away. My words are trapped in my head. They speak to me."

"I know," I pull him, he spills towards me. "What do they say?"

"They say my anger is trapped, it's lost in my head. The No Souls are haunting me Bunches. Their nasty words are killing me."

Dan's hearing them. The No Souls have become real.

"How do you know I called them the No Souls?" I ask, my eyes searching his looking for the truth.

"I know everything about you Bunches. I can read you and them too. It's a gift, or perhaps it's a punishment. I don't know."

We stay for a while as if absorbing much needed energy from the thunderclaps. I know it is a risky tactic but still we remain. The nervous energy in my body is pulsating, growing with each thunderclap.

At last I say, "Can you turn it off? Your gift?"

"I try to, but sometimes I can't help but eavesdrop into other peoples' minds."

I nod as if this is just an everyday conversation. But my tummy flips as it accepts that my boyfriend is a psychic poetic.

"Come on, we better go, before we get soaked," I urge.

"Okay," he replies. He stands up letting raindrops drip like tears from his black hair.

We walk unsure whether to run; I drag him towards safety. My house, my front door, the lightning is kind to us. I fiddle in my bag to try to find my house keys. I locate my key ring, a huge purple question mark, and turn the key in the door leaving the lighting to chase some other lost soul. We take our coats off in the hallway, dripping water on the floor. I take his hand and lead him upstairs. He is so silent that it scares me. I pull a chair back and motion for him to sit down. As I open my cupboard drawer, I look for a pen, and a notebook. I place the pen in his hand. He looks at me blankly, I turn to a page in the notebook as it lays pleading in front of him.

The notebook has never known ink. Its pages are pristine.

"Write," I command. I am surprised by the forcefulness of my voice.

He grabs his hair and stabs the page as if he hates it. I let him.

"Try," I coax.

He writes one word: *love.* It fills the page, but it looks wobbly.

Tears spill from his eyes as he writes another word: *you.*

Followed by: *My ghosts are free.*

I'm better, 'cause of you.

We hug, our tears mingling with the.raindrops.

The thunder calms.

"I know what to call you." I say.

Dan smiles.

"Mine," we both whisper at the same time. And then we kiss. The kiss is so poetic, we will never be alone again.

The virus failed to kill us. The bullies will not win.

Shopping Hell—Flash Fiction

It's a Friday night, the weekends coming! What a joke. It is almost impossible to keep note of the day of the week, but I do. I have a calendar on my wall and I mark off each day. Fridays, Saturdays and Sundays I write party time in bold, colourful letters to cheer myself up.

Weekend means treats. But, I've run out of any food so I must go to the supermarket.

I dread what the queue might be like.

I can't believe my luck when I see no one waiting. Not one person. The yellow barriers are weaving, snakes turning and twisting to keep customers where we should be. Controlled. Safe. Apart.

Each time I buy food, I become more afraid. It's so eerie, you can sense the fear. I'm afraid to touch anything. I pray I don't see someone I know. It has become better to avoid or pretend that I don't see others. Social distancing has become social avoidance.

I'm done quick, I don't even bother with a basket, my purchases are piled high, one ready meal on top of the other, stacked high. Sweet and sour chicken, sticky red sauce clinging to the plastic, glutinous rice stuffed to the lid, and a portion of gooey spare ribs.

Within minutes I am at the nearest till. For a moment my fear subsides as I see a familiar face, the vicar talking to the check out assistant. He appears so serene. His hair is brushed and neat, his smile genuine. I wish I could be like him. I wonder if I should have gone to church, prayed to God. He chats to the check out lady as if it is a normal day, wishes her well and leaves with a smile.

I'm still thinking of the vicar, how he seems to have no fear of death. In a stupor I forget to social distance. The lady at the till commands me to step back. I do, but I can never get used to this.

It hurts.

She softens her tone, realising I am close to tears, she begins chatting to me caressing my fear away. The topic: our prime minister who has become infected with coronavirus. Apparently, Boris Johnson had been shaking hands. She suggested he should have hip bumped instead. I almost smile.

I never shake hands. I'm glad of that.

I have no bag, just a purse and bare arms. I pay with a contactless card. It's safer that way.

As I leave the store, I clutch the ready meals. I move in the wrong direction and the security guard asks me to follow the snake trail towards the right. His job today is to herd, not to handcuff thieves. I recognise a mother of a girl I used to go to primary school with; she glances at me but doesn't say anything. Perhaps she doesn't recognise me? I'm lying to myself. Now a line of people are standing waiting at a distance from each other, some wearing masks, others gloves, some both.

I feel them looking at me, wishing they were me, leaving.

Shopping Hell (2)—Flash fiction

A woman is standing in front of me in the supermarket queue. She's young, barely twenty, wearing a bright red jacket, a face mask, her hair is dark, her eyes accusatory. Turning her head, her body twists, she glares at me, her body language screams you are too close, as if I am invading her territory. Her glossy red jacket screams help! I'm staying away from her, following the social distancing rules, but still it is not enough. She fears me, her eyes peer at me above her mask and I know this is true. I hope and pray she will stay well. She is a similar age to my daughters, but fear has made her an anxious stranger.

Student Flat (Family—Flash Fiction)

The announcement of Lockdown came as I'd been packing my luggage, getting ready to return home to my parents in Scotland.

Now I'm stuck in doors in my student flat with a bunch of people who aren't willing to isolate, wash dishes, use toilet paper, or clean their hands every day. Two of the guys eat off the table, no plate. Can you imagine? I'm living in a zoo.

My chances are a lottery no one wants to play. If I'd left yesterday before the lockdown I could be talking to my mum at home. Instead, I'm here wishing I was there. Who knows where I will be safer? There is no safer.

I Skype mum that night. She's crying, really upset I can't get home to be with them, but glad I am at a safe distance as dad is ill. I put a brave face on, but inside I am crying. What will become of him? What will become of us, I wonder?

Mum brushes away her tears, my sister joins in the Skype session. Dad is ill in bed with an unconfirmed illness. There are no coronavirus testing kits available for the public at the moment, not unless you are sick enough that it is obvious what you have. In other words, you are already admitted to hospital and gasping to breathe. Dad has a mild illness, he could have the flu, he could have any other virus, or he could have the virus.

Even during our Skype call, my sister Jess senses my isolation and fear. She smiles and says, "Don't worry. Dad's okay, he's not got any breathing difficulties. He had a cough, and a raised temperature, but no fever. He's isolating. Mum and I are keeping well and cleaning like crazy!"

"Ha Ha! You cleaning Jess? That I would love to see."

"I hope those dirty devils in your flat are cleaning up?" asks mum, her voice rising with anxiety.

"Not exactly. But I'm wearing gloves and cleaning too."

"Glad to hear it," says mum. "Tell those filthy so and so's to help."

"I'll do that," I lie, knowing the only way to make them help would be to point a pistol at them.

"What else have you been doing?" asks Jen.

"Watching TV, trying out new recipes with whatever ingredients I can find. Dancing around the flat."

"Same," says Jen. "Not dancing but keeping fit. Hey, Luce, I've got a great idea. You know how you've always wanted to be a blogger. Why not give it a go? If not now, when sis?"

I wish I could hug her. She's always been the strong one, even though she's a year younger than me, she is the tower of **we can do this**.

Mum smiles. "Yes, that's a wonderful idea Jen," she moves to hug my little sister and then remembers she can't. Not whilst dad is ill. She blows her a kiss instead.

Jen blows one back, I join in. We kiss, and kiss and kiss, a dizzying flurry of on-line kisses.

I am silent for a while, knowing that Jen is right. But what kind of blogger will I be? I know the answer, it is simple, a mental health blogger. Even our strongest will need help.

Stay At Home (Trigger Warning.)

Rich lays in bed.

His wife has just put his profile picture up on Facebook with the caption 'Stay at home.' His breathing is laboured, his thoughts petrified. What has he brought into his house? His wife, children and new baby, what has he done?

Regret flows through his veins, entwining with the progress of the deadly virus. He acknowledges his failings, softly whispering for forgiveness to a God he never knew he had.

His thoughts rage, condemning himself for his stupidity. He's an idiot who carried on as normal, mixing in groups, laughing at the virus, putting up funny jokes on his Facebook profile page. Now the virus *has* him, it is gripping his chest, punching his lungs for his stupidity and carelessness. It is laughing at him.

Next door he hears his baby daughter crying. A tear spills from his eyes. He can't get up to feed her, he can't hold her in his arms. His wife's footsteps come rushing, her voice soft and gentle as she tries to calm their baby down while he is certain that her terrified heart beats to a tune he cannot touch.

The baby is quietened. He guesses she's been fed, nappy changed, tucked back under the covers. Safe. Or is she? He can't see his family as they are in the living room next door to his isolated bedroom, but he knows his wife has opened her Facebook page to read more grim accounts of death. His photo has been shared again with the caption begging their friends and family to, "*Please* Stay at Home."

The word *please* shouts but will people listen?

Fighting through fever, he tries to focus, to listen for his son. Where is he? He struggles to hear. He fears that he might notice a new sound, a cough, perhaps, a dry, wheezing sound.

Nothing. Not a sound.

Instead, he coughs, his temperature racing.

Then he hears his son's voice, scared. "What's wrong, mummy. Why are you crying?"

"It's okay, Jonny," his wife soothes. "Look, I'm keeping busy, cleaning your Lego, then you can play."

"Where's Daddy?" asks his son.

"He's in bed, Jonny."

"But, I want to play with him," Jonny whines.

"He's sick Jonny, we have to let Daddy rest."

He can't see his wife, his sweetheart, his son, or his newborn baby and this breaks his heart. But he knows how rigorously his wife will clean their son's toys. How she will pop each piece of Lego in the sterilisation liquid before drying them meticulously.

A mother's love is unstoppable.

But he can hear his wife. "Go play," she says, sighing.

His son shouts, "Yay," as if it is a normal day. "Can I go to the park?"

"No," his wife yells. Then her voice pierces the air with even more urgency. It is a knife to his heart. "Don't put things in your mouth."

His son is crying. "Sorry, mummy."

"Oh, darling, I didn't mean to shout at you."

His son sniffs, and his wife consoles.

Rich continues to listen, but he hears nothing. It is silent for a time. He imagines his son building a fortress to keep the virus out. His wife watching him, marvelling at their young son, wondering who he will become. A scientist who will cure deadly viruses. Or a doctor who will save patients.

By now Rich is struggling to breathe, but he can't shout for help. He can't risk infecting his loved ones. He has to be a grown up. This isn't the flu. This isn't the sniffles. He knows that now, but perhaps it is too late. If they stay away, perhaps they will be safe.

The virus will decide.

Paper Hugs (Family—Positivity)

It's hard for the kids. They can't see their friends, or go out to play as normal. So, mums and dads have to get creative.

We tried a new game today, but games have rules. The most important ritual is to wash your hands for twenty seconds with soap and water. We chose rainbow soap, and we sang a special song.

It goes like this:

Clean your grubby hands,

Clean your grubby hands,

Wash away the snotty goo,

Brother, sister, mum and dad,

You and you and you and you!

Scrub your fingers in between

Up and over itchy palms

Soap all over funny thumbs

Brother, sister, mum and dad,

You and you and you and you!

It always makes the children laugh and helps them to clean their hands properly.

Dad takes a break from working to join in the washing hands ritual too.

We all laugh. Sometimes dad changes the song lyrics and instead of saying goo, he says poo instead. That makes us all laugh some more.

Then he blows us all a kiss and goes back to work in his office. His office is now in our house. He shuts the door and leaves me in charge.

They look at me as if to say what's next mum.

Then one of them pipes up, "What shall we do now?"

Luckily, today I have an answer. "Let's make hugs."

"But, mummy, you can't make hugs!" says my son, Jack, his chubby boy's cheeks reminding me how young and precious he is.

"Yes, you can," I reply, as I move toward the craft cupboard. "We are going to make paper hugs to send to our friends."

I place two large pieces of paper on the floor. Libby lies on the first piece of paper.

"I'm like an angel," she giggles, her arms outstretched, her blue eyes twinkling.

I cut out the shape of her head and upper body, and then I do the same for her little brother. Then they colour them in with felt-tip pens.

After they've finished, I hand them paper and pencils to write some little notes to go with the hugs.

My son's note reads: Hi Danny… I miss you. Hug foo you. See you after nastie sickie thing goes. Jack.

His spelling needs some work!

My daughters says: Annie. A big hug for you. It's the biggest and best hug. Send me one too. Pleae. Miss you. Lots….Libby.

Libby's note with such neat writing and few spelling mistakes makes me smile.

Then I write the address on their masterpieces to send to their friends. It's the little things that make a difference. It's nice to see them smile.

A few days later we receive some hugs back. The children are so excited. They stick them up on their bedroom walls and everything is sunny for a day.

Killers Mustn't Win

I stood by the platform waiting for my train, my mask tight against my face. A man jeered at me, his lips twisted in a cruel grimace. I moved back.

"I have something for you," he smiled as he spat. I felt his wet spittle on my exposed skin. I screamed, frantically searching for a tissue to erase death from my face.

Onlookers stared, their hearts bound by fear as their masks sagged. He wiped his mouth, licking his cruel lips. Tears streamed from my eyes. I vowed to fight this virus; killers mustn't win.

Two Spits For The NHS

Annie remembered the night when her neighbours went out to cheer the NHS, how touched she had felt then. It had made her cry.

Now, one spit and then another straight in her face. She had asked her attacker to observe the rules, not to come too close on his bike, but instead he had acted in such a way, perhaps to infect her—if he had the virus.

She'd just completed her ten-hour shift, exhausted and been rewarded like this. She rushed home crying, ran a shower and immersed her skin under the jets of hot water for hours, shaking and petrified. What would happen if her attacker infected her with the virus? What then?

She was proud of her uniform. She was proud of the NHS. But who would take her shift if she became ill?

If she continued to stay well, she vowed to bring a change of clothes to work, so she would never be targeted again.

A birthday poem

For poor

Vincent Van Gogh

I wrote a mirror Cinquain poem about The Spring Garden painting stolen from the Singer Laren Museum in the Netherlands on Van Gogh's birthday, 30th March.

What strikes me about this is the calculated nastiness of:

❖ Stealing the painting on the artist's birthday.

❖ Particularly as Van Gogh never achieved recognition during his lifetime, tormented by poverty, mental health problems and ultimately suicide.

❖ Timing the robbery to occur on the First day of Spring.

❖ When the world is struggling with a terrible virus which is killing thousands of people. What a calculated act.

Vincent

Van Gogh's birthday

Marred by show off robbers

An opportunist crime caper

So sad

More so

'Cause Vincent didn't get his dues

Virus villains stealing

Priceless Beauty

In Spring

To find out more about the robbery -

Van Gogh painting Spring Garden stolen from Dutch museum:
https://www.bbc.co.uk/news/world-europe-52097246

https://www.independent.co.uk/arts-entertainment/art/news/van-gogh-spring-garden-stolen-painting-netherlands-singer-laren-a9436036.html

A Letter to Van Gogh From The World

Dear Sir,

On this your birthday, Monday 30ᵗʰ March 2020, I have sad news to impart to you. It is with regret that I must inform you that your beautiful painting has been stolen from the Singer Laren Museum in the Netherlands. We will do our utmost to retrieve the Spring Garden and bring these despicable criminals to justice.

"Thieves broke into the museum around 3.15am on Monday morning and stole the artwork featuring the vicarage garden in Nuenen painted in the spring of 1884, titled Spring Garden. The painting, estimated to be worth up to £5m, was on loan to the Singer Laren museum from the Groninger Museum. No other art pieces were burgled."

Kind regards,

Dearest World (less the Scumbags.)

Dearest World (Less the Thieves, disreputable villains, and scumbags.)

My dearly departed soul is touched by your message. How dare the villainous scum! My beautiful pastoral painting, Spring Garden, which I created in (1884) touched by foul hands.

I am turning and turning in my grave!

BUT…Why did you fail to keep my darling Spring Garden safe? My precious painting! It's bad enough that the Groninger Museum loaned my painting to the Sanger.

And now this. My art is worth riches beyond my wildest dreams, but I have no need of money. I am a ghost. A bitter ghost. Such irony, the painting is worth 5 million, or thereabouts, I cannot imagine such a sum of money! The injustice. After years of mental torment, poverty and trauma. I drank, starved and suffered for my art, I even cut off my ear. At thirty-seven, I committed suicide.

Have they no heart?

I will meet the perpetrators of this atrocity in the afterlife.

They better be afraid. Why was no one watching over my dearest Spring Garden?

Catch the villains! This better not be some kind of publicity stunt.

Yours distraught,

Flaming mad,

Vincent Van Gogh

Letter From The World

Dear Van Gogh,

We are in the grips of a terrible sickness, which is killing thousands of people worldwide. An illness of enormous proportions.

We are scared.

The World

Vincent Van Gogh To The World

Dearest World,

Ah, it is man's lot to suffer. I fear for you. I wish I could paint again. Human suffering should always be expressed in brushstrokes. But your modern world. The madness of it. I cannot begin to comprehend. There is no point in riches—as I have no need for money anymore. Death has stripped away everything.

Everything but my wishes. PLEASE keep my dearest paintings safe.

OR, I SWEAR I WILL COME BACK AND HAUNT YOU!

Catch the thieving wretches! Or the sickness will reach them first!

I swear this by God Almighty, he has my ear.

Vincent.

Love Affair (Post Virus)

Annie glanced at her scrawny husband. A glance was all it took. He couldn't lift her, no carried wife could she ever be. No threshold over which she could be taken. Adam was different. His different scared her. She couldn't help but imagine Adam lifting her onto his shoulders and running to the ocean, his bare skin wet with the salty water, his hard, taut muscles flexing. What would happen thereafter? Would he leave her to the fishes, or scoop her up with dreamy kisses? She knew what she would become: a carried Jezebel; perhaps she'd like that more.

She stared at the text. *Meet me by the waterfront.* She stared and wondered, what to do?

She knew the answer even before she typed it. Her impulsive reply, *I'll be there in ten minutes.*

Her husband Ian lay on the settee, his mouth wide open, snoring. No need to trouble him with the details. She left a hand-written message: Gone to meet a friend for lunch, I'll be back soon.

She didn't stop to apply her makeup just in case her husband woke up. Instead, she popped her lipstick and mascara into her handbag. She'd stop and beautify herself later in the toilet near the seafront.

Parking was easy. The car park was nearly empty. She walked down the path to the sea. It was cold and deserted in the toilet. The cracked mirror made it very difficult to apply her makeup. She did what she could and then she walked to the seafront. And waited.

In the distance she spotted a seagull, it swooped high in the sky and then landed on the raised edge of the path near her. She swore it was posing for her, so stationery it sat, as if it wanted to be photographed.

She pulled her mobile phone out of her bag and snapped its picture. Captured. She was so engrossed that she didn't hear footsteps, or hear his approach.

"Hi," he said as he swooped down to gather her in a hug. He was tall, his body lean. She breathed heavily into his chest, absorbing his masculine scent.

The seagull flew off as if jealous of this intrusion.

She watched it go.

"What are you thinking?" he asked, kissing her cheek.

"I'm thinking I'd like to fly away with you."

"You'll never do that," he said.

"Why?"

"Because you like your cake and eat it," he laughed, his blue eyes twinkling.

"What about you, what do you want?"

"I'll settle to be your crumbs on the side. As long as you promise to lick the plate."

She raised her face to kiss him. He tasted of sea salt and farm honey. Sweet and sour.

They clung together for an age, lips refusing to part. Her lipstick gone, taken by the pressure of his lips.

She would leave her husband. There was nothing else left. Their love had flown away, taken by the virus, which in turn had taught her that she couldn't stay. If her lover was to be her crumbs, she would accept that. Time would tell whether he would become her cake.

Domestic Abuse—Triggering

All round the world there are women like me. To the outside world, my husband and I don't appear any different from any other couple. He is handsome, successful, confident, and so good at hiding who he really is, or who he becomes when he is angry or stressed. And I am good at hiding my fear, bruises and injuries.

I live in a small town in France which you've probably never heard of. I'd rather not tell you what my name is, or which town we live in as I'd prefer to keep my anonymity.

Last week, I heard our government has set up an "alert system" in pharmacies nationwide, where victims of domestic abuse could discreetly ask the pharmacist to call the police by asking for "mask 19."

I'm particularly vulnerable as I am pregnant. When my partner slapped me in the face and threatened me with a knife, I knew it was the end. I had to escape. I had to chance it, to go to a pharmacy and get help. But I knew if I went with him I'd lose my nerve. I had to find a way to get out of the house without him.

The morning after the assault he'd been all conciliatory, making me breakfast in bed and telling me how much he loved me and the baby.

After I'd eaten breakfast, I popped to the toilet. I stood by the sink, my knees buckling under me, and for a moment I thought I'd be sick.

Trembling, I walked back into our bedroom.

"I need to call the doctor," I said, unable to stop my hands shaking, I placed them behind my back.

"Why?" he asked, his smile fading. His hidden hands were resting under the sheets clenching ready to punch.

"I have some bleeding. I should get advice about whether it is normal to bleed at this time in my pregnancy." I hunched forward.

He released his clenched his hands, mortified, full of remorse, scared that we'd lose the baby. Then he said, "I'm sure it must just be the stress of the coronavirus."

What a bastard.

I knew stress. I lived with stress every day. He was my stress.

Then came the hardest part, when I told him I had to go to the pharmacy to get the sanitary towels for the light bleeding.

I could feel my trembling intensifying. Doubting whether he would believe me, whether his fists would lash out.

"I'll come with you," he said, pulling the bed sheet away from him.

"No, it's okay," I replied. "I don't want to expose you to more germs than you need to. I'll be quick, I'll go to the nearest pharmacy and come straight back." I moved forward and kissed him on the cheek, the touch of his skin made me wretch. I turned my face away hiding my reaction from him.

The bastard agreed. I knew he would.

He's a liar, he doesn't love me, or our baby. All he cares about is himself.

The corona virus doesn't love anyone either. It is a ruthless ball, thrown from person to person, sometimes it hits its target, landing with a mild slap and sometimes it hits hard, or kills. Each time I feel my baby kick, I am glad that I chose to protect her from those punches.

I have to protect her from him and from the virus.

It's taken me to this moment to know this.

At last we are safe. Pray God the virus stays away.

Granddad is Coming Home

(Flash Fiction—Uplifting)

Grandma couldn't believe it; her husband had survived.

At eighty-seven he was in the *at risk group*. Someone was looking after him and it wasn't just the NHS! She looked at his photo in the news, walking arm-in-arm with an NHS worker. He was wearing a face mask, and yet he looked like he could take on the world. The nurse's face glowed with joy, happy to share some good news about his recovery from COVID19 pneumonia. The image was shared all over the world, gobbled up by viewers desperate for some cheerful news.

For a moment Grandma pondered the strangeness of life. What was God's plan in all of this? She had no idea but her heart filled with happiness at the thought of her dear husband coming home.

Thank you for reading

This Is Lockdown

During lockdown I discovered several reviews for my books. I mention it here because reviews mean so much to authors. They make us smile even in sad times.

If you enjoyed *This Is Lockdown*, I would be very grateful if you would consider leaving a review for the collection.

And also I hope you will find many new authors to follow, read and review!

Thank you in anticipation

ABOUT M J MALLON

My favourite genres to write are fantasy YA, Paranormal, Ghost and Horror Stories, various forms of poetry and flash fiction. I celebrate the spiritual realm, love of nature and all things magical, mystical, and mysterious at my blog home: https://mjmallon.com I'd describe myself as a reading, blogging and photography enthusiast!

My alter ego is MJ—Mary Jane from Spider-man. I love superheroes! I was born on the 17th of November in Lion City: Singapore, (a passionate Scorpio, with the Chinese Zodiac sign a lucky rabbit,) second child and only daughter to my parents Paula and Ronald. I grew up in a mountainous court in the Peak District in Hong Kong with my elder brother Donald.

It's rumoured that I now live in the Venice of Cambridge, with my six-foot hunk of a Rock God husband. My two enchanted daughters often come back to see me with a cheery smile.

When I'm not writing, I eat exotic delicacies while belly dancing, or surf to the far reaches of the moon. To chill out, I practise yoga or mindfulness. If the mood takes me, I snorkel with mermaids, or sign up for idyllic holidays with the Chinese Unicorn, whose magnificent voice sings like a thousand wind chimes. I am a member of The Society of Children's Writers and Book Illustrators—SCBWI.

Also By M J Mallon

Kyrosmagica Publishing

YA Fantasy: The Curse of Time Book1 Bloodstone

https://mybook.to/TheCurseofTime

Poetry, Prose and Photography: Mr. Sagittarius

http://mybook.to/MrSagittarius

Available on Amazon kindle, Kindle unlimited and paperback

Short Stories in Anthologies:

Bestselling horror compilations

Nightmareland compiled by Dan Alatorre

"Scrabble Boy" (Short Story)

Spellbound compiled by Dan Alatorre

"The Twisted Sisters" (Short Story)

Ghostly Rites 2019 compiled by Claire Plaisted

"Dexter's Creepy Caverns" (Short Story)

Ghostly Rites 2020 compiled by Claire Plaisted

"No. 1 Coven Lane" (Short Story)

Coming in 2021…

YA Fantasy:

The Curse of Time Book 2 Golden Healer

Poetry, and Flash Fiction collection:

Do what you Love

Wings of Fire compiled by Dan Alatorre

"The Great Pottoo" (Short Story)

Blog: https://mjmallon.com

Twitter: @Marjorie_Mallon and @curseof_time

Amazon Author Page:
https://www.amazon.co.uk/M-J-Mallon/e/B074CGNK4L/

Goodreads:
https://www.goodreads.com/author/show/17064826.M_J_Mallon

Facebook: https://www.facebook.com/mjmallonauthor/

Instagram: https://www.instagram.com/mjmallonauthor/

Bookbub: https://www.bookbub.com/authors/m-j-mallon

Authors, Bloggers Rainbow Support Club #ABRSC:
https://www.facebook.com/groups/1829166787333493/

www.ingramcontent.com/pod-product-compliance
Lightning Source LLC
Chambersburg PA
CBHW021106130626
46554CB00002B/557